OUR AMERICAN COUSIN
The Play That Changed History

A Modern Reading Edition
Edited and Introduced
by
WELFORD DUNAWAY TAYLOR

■ *TOM TAYLOR*

BEACHAM PUBLISHING, INC.
W A S H I N G T O N , D . C .

92–138

Library of Congress
Cataloguing-in-Publication Data

Taylor, Tom, 1817–1880.
    Our American Cousin : the play that changed history /
Tom Taylor. — A modern reading ed. / edited and introduced by
Welford Dunaway Taylor.
        p. 24 cm.
    Includes bibliographical references.
    ISBN 0–933833–20–2 : $18.00
    I. Taylor, Welford Dunaway.   II. Title.
                                    PR5549.T4A75   1990
    822'.8—dc20   90–42793

Book and Cover Design by Amanda Mott

ISBN 0–933833–20–2
Printed in the United States of America
First Printing, September 1990

For
the Taylors of Caroline, neighbors of the Garretts

CONTENTS

▪ Introduction ▪

For Americans who had lived through the Civil War, April 14, 1865 began as an extraordinary day. In addition to being Good Friday, it marked the fourth anniversary of the surrender of Fort Sumter, the first military engagement of the war. But this year it was part of a week-long victory celebration, for General Lee had surrendered to General Grant at Appomattox just five days before (on Palm Sunday). By midnight, however, the day was marked forever by a single tragic event: President Abraham Lincoln had been mortally wounded by an assassin while watching a play at Ford's Theatre.

Walt Whitman maintained that the assassination overshadowed the entire four years of civil strife.[1] Indeed, the impact of this mad act has proved so sweeping that many of the important individuals and events surrounding it have been eclipsed. Prominent among them is the play which the President was enjoying when John Wilkes Booth delivered his mortal wound. To most modern-day readers *Our American Cousin* is little more than a title and its author, Tom Taylor, simply a forgotten name. In spite of that fact, Taylor's play was one of the most popular and durable in the nineteenth century repertoire.

From its New York premiere in 1858 forward, it consistently delighted and amused American and British audiences, and it continued to do so long after the ill-starred Washington production. Its basic plot of a cloddish American thrust among his aris-

1

tocratic English kin contained elements that reflected the expansionist mood of nineteenth century America. These characteristics, often found in melodramas of the time, included love-at-first-sight, the punishment of a deceitful villain, selfless sacrifice, and a happy-ever-after ending. But unlike many such plays, *Our American Cousin* features several characters of unique distinction. In addition to the "cousin," Asa Trenchard, there is the shrewd but engaging Florence Trenchard and the pompous aristocrat Lord Dundreary, whose fame became part of theatrical folklore.

The sudden fusing of this farcical comedy with tragedy, which underscores the ironic history of both the assassination and of *Our American Cousin*, began with two chains of events on April 3, 1865—events that initially seemed unrelated. On that day Richmond, Virginia, the Confederate capital, was evacuated by its government. It was an inevitable prelude to General Lee's surrender at Appomattox, (which would occur six days later). In Washington the news of General Grant's victory over Lee created a mood which contrasted markedly with the sombreness of Holy Week. The President was haled and congratulated on all sides. On Tuesday evening he spoke from an open window at the White House to tumultuous applause and joyful band music. On Thursday evening, April 13, the euphoria of victory was repeated when the city became "one blaze of glorious light"[2] from a fireworks display and from the turned-up gaslights in many public buildings. In the upper windows of the War Department reflectors, activated by the beams of calcium torches, proclaimed "GRANT."

April 3 had likewise marked the arrival of the popular comedienne Laura Keene in Washington. Having toured widely during the war years, she was beginning a two-week engagement with the Ford's Theatre stock company. She was to play roles in English classics such as Goldsmith's *She Stoops to Conquer* and Sheridan's *The School for Scandal*—parts for which she was well known on the theatrical circuit. But she was perhaps more celebrated for her portrayal of Florence Trenchard, the female lead in Tom Taylor's *Our American Cousin*, which she had played "upwards of 1,000 nights."[3] She had also been the first producer of the play, and still retained ownership. The Ford's production of April 14 was to be her final Washington performance. It would also be her "benefit" (i.e. she would receive a share of the gate as a bonus).

Facts concerning the Lincolns' decision to attend this production of *Our American Cousin* are incomplete and at times contradictory; however, certain key points in the process are well documented. On April 13 General and Mrs. Grant arrived in Washington in mid-afternoon. Their destination was Philadelphia, but the General needed to confer with Secretary of War Stanton. The Grants' unexpected appearance at the Willard Hotel caused a flurry of excitement. The visit was also an apparent surprise to the Lincolns, who hurriedly made plans to honor the general. At some point between the Grants' arrival on April 13 and mid-morning of April 14, the President invited the General and his lady to attend the theatre with him and Mrs Lincoln. Apparently the President offered the invitation because the hostility between the First Lady and Mrs. Grant was long-standing, and had erupted publicly just a few days before at City Point, Virginia.

At this point the known details become confusing. A new play, *Aladdin, or the Wonderful Lamp,* was being presented at Grover's Theatre (the National Theatre) and C. D. Hess, the theatre manager, had sent the Lincolns an invitation on the 13th for the following evening. According to Leonard Grover, the proprietor, Lincoln sent back a handwritten note accepting the invitation for himself and his son, Tad. He did this early on the morning of the 14th.[4] *Our American Cousin*, announced as Ford's production for the 14th, was an old play, one which had been produced in Washington several times over the last few years, and Lincoln had probably seen Laura Keene in the leading female role the last time it was given.[5] However, before 10:30 a.m.—in advance of an 11:00 a.m. Cabinet meeting—Lincoln dispatched a messenger to Ford's for the purpose of reserving the State Box on the second tier for the Lincoln-Grant party, as General Grant had verbally accepted the invitation. Why Lincoln changed his mind and decided upon *Our American Cousin* at Ford's over *Aladdin* at Grover's remains a puzzling question. Perhaps he thought a play about a rough-and-ready American would be more appealing to a conquering hero than one dealing with Oriental exoticism. Perhaps it was the combined appeal of a celebrated actress, a popular play, a farewell performance, and a benefit. But this is only speculation.

It is certain, however, that the idea seemed ill-fated from the outset. Grant, always ill at ease at public functions, desired to complete his business as soon as possible and continue on his journey. Although he had initially accepted the President's invitation, he formally regretted early on Friday afternoon and left Washington soon thereafter with Mrs. Grant.[6] Over the next few hours several other invitations were politely declined. Lincoln "felt inclined to give up the whole thing,"[7] but this was not easily done. Announcements of the Lincoln-Grant appearance had been made in the afternoon editions of two newspapers. Mrs. Lincoln felt that cancelling would further disappoint a public already denied the opportunity to see Grant. At the last minute two guests were added, Major Henry R. Rathbone (the President's military aide) and his fiance, Miss Clara Harris (daughter of Senator Ira Harris of New York, who held the Senate seat vacated by William H. Seward, Lincoln's Secretary of State).

Once the State Box was reserved, theatre personnel responded appropriately. The partition separating two small boxes on the second tier was removed, creating a single, more commodious space. James T. Ford, the business manager, borrowed flags from the Treasury Department, which were attached to the front of the box, festooning a gilt-framed print of George Washington. Furniture was set in place, the major piece being the President's trademark, a high-backed rocker with arms rests. H. Polkinhorn, a local printer, interrupted the running of handbills to include part of the lyrics to a new song, H.B. Phillips' "Honor to Our Soldiers," for which William Withers, director of the Ford orchestra, had written music.[8] Laura Keene had lent her personal piano for the singing of this patriotic number, and she would decide when it would be performed.[9] Since Grant was expected,

Ford's normal capacity of 1,700 would doubtlessly be swelled to 2,300 or perhaps even more. This meant adding several hundred straight-back chairs.

At about 3:00 p.m., as rehearsals were completed and as stage carpenters were storing scenery, a familiar visitor arrived at Ford's. A popular actor and a congenial colleague, John Wilkes Booth frequented both Ford's and Grover's theatres, as each gave him freedom of the house. He routinely received his mail at Ford's when he was in Washington and he could, and frequently did, walk into either establishment at any time he pleased. Everyone from managers, to actors, to stage hands knew him, and his visits to Ford's were often followed by drinks at Peter Taltavul's Star Saloon, which adjoined the theatre building.

But Booth's appearance on this Good Friday afternoon was no ordinary social call, nor was it his first that day—or his last. It was, however, a crucial visit for, although brief, it enabled him to complete the final details in a long and erratic scheme which involved an undetermined number of people. For more than a century and a quarter historical analysts have argued whether John Wilkes Booth was the mastermind of a small conspiracy to murder Abraham Lincoln or the instrument of a larger, more elaborate plot orchestrated by the Confederate government. In 1988 an imposing new study, some ten years in the making, appeared, arguing persuasively for the latter possibility.[10]

Whatever its provenance, Booth's plan to assassinate Abraham Lincoln on Friday, April 14 was not perfected until that very day. This is verified by the fact that on the previous evening, after learning that the Acting Manager of Grover's Theatre was to issue the President a special invitation for the 14th, Booth dispatched a messenger to purchase a nearby box for him. During the forenoon of April 14, he went to Grover's himself (doubtlessly to advance plans for his attack), only to find that Lincoln had regretted the invitation.

About noon Harry Ford, treasurer of Ford's Theatre, was standing at one of the front entrances (which faced 10th Street) as Booth walked down from the corner of F Street. The two began to talk and joke, and Booth sent a theatre worker inside for his mail. It was during this conversation that he learned, from Ford, that Lincoln planned to attend the evening performance of *Our American Cousin*. Booth did not leave the theatre immediately. Instead, he went upstairs.

Ford's Theatre was a relatively new building, having opened on August 27, 1863. Since that time Booth had come to know it well—as an actor on its boards, as a friend to its various personnel, and as a frequenter of its interior. It was a small building, measuring only 72 by 110 feet, but it contained various levels, which denoted several categories of seats. The President would occupy the State Box on the second tier, near the dress circle. A small staircase ascended from the left of the downstairs lobby to the second tier. Here an outside door led into an alcove from which one gained access to the boxes.

In addition to knowing the interior configuration of Ford's, Booth knew the play which would be presented there in a few hours. The historian Jim Bishop has constructed a plausible account of Booth's thoughts as he considered how to integrate the design of the theatre and the play into his diabolical scheme:

> He was acquainted with almost every line of *Our American Cousin.* In the box, with no gas lights on, he was cloaked in daytime gloom and he sat watching, thinking— who knows? He looked from the ledge of the box to the stage, and he knew that he had made bigger leaps in *Macbeth.* He could not plan to run back through the dress circle because, the moment the act was accomplished, it could be expected that the people in the theatre would be in bedlam. Besides, he would have to stab the guard outside the little white door in case of challenge. It was better to stick to the original idea, to jump to the stage, run across toward the Green Room, and out the back door. If he had a horse there, waiting, escape could be fairly easy.[11]

Some forty-five minutes after Booth talked with Harry Ford in front of the theatre, he was seen by Harry's brother, James, on the corner of 10th and E, bound for C Street and Pumphrey's livery stable. When Booth returned to Ford's at 3:00 p.m., just as the rehearsal for *Our American Cousin* was concluding, his plan was all but formed. There remained only the arrangements for securing the horse he had rented from Pumphrey's. This was easily achieved with the aid of some of his stage-hand friends.

Perhaps the key to the success of Booth's scheme was its simplicity. It called for no alteration in the normal course of life, and it aroused no suspicions. No one at the theatre would be surprised to see him during a performance. There was nothing unusual about leaving a horse in the public alley at the rear. Moreover, he had determined that the play itself afforded an ideal moment for making his move. There was a point in Act III, Scene 2 when a single actor would be on the stage, at far left. This is the scene in which the "American Cousin," Asa Trenchard, exposes the hypocrisy of Mrs. Mountchessington and her daughter. They exit, and he calls after them. This moment, one of the funniest in the play, always drew prolonged laughter. Tonight it would be his moment. Still, he would have to act quickly and decisively and, to some extent, trust luck. What of the guard usually posted outside the alcove door? Would he be in place tonight? Booth must wait. Meantime, he would let events evolve naturally.

And so they seemed to do. Between 5:00 and 6:00 p.m., Booth brought the lively mare from Pumphreys and left her in a stable he rented behind the theatre, according to plan. A little past 7:30, following several last-minute delays, the Lincoln carriage left the White House. At 7:45 the performance began with an orchestral overture. After stopping for Major Rathbone and Miss Harris, the carriage arrived at the theatre about 8:30. By this time the play was well into its lengthy first scene. Florence Trenchard (Laura Keene), Lord Dundreary (E. A. Emerson), and Mrs. Mountchessington (Mrs. Muzzy) were on stage engaging in an absurd game of word-play. It proved an ideal moment for the clever actress to interpose an announcement of the President's arrival.

"That wath a joke, that wath," Dundreary lisped. "Where's the joke?" Florence asked, and Mrs. Mountchessington answered, "No." "She don't see it," began Dundreary. Florence quickly interrupted with an ad-libbed line, "Anybody can see *that!*" and pointed to the Presidential box. William Withers struck up "Hail to the Chief," and there was vigorous applause. Again, in Act II, Scene 2, another opportunity for an ad-lib line presented itself, when Dundreary attempted to seat the "delicate" Georgina just outside the dairy. "I am afraid of the draft here," she said. He replied, "Don't be alarmed, for there is no more draft." Once more the applause was "long and loud."[12]

About 9:00 p.m. Booth appeared at the rear door of the theatre, leading the mare he had rented. He asked Ned Spangler, a stage hand, to hold the horse for him. Spangler could not leave his post; instead he had J. L. DeBonay, another stage-hand, summon "Peanuts" Burroughs (a youth who ran errands at the theatre) to hold the reins. Booth then asked DeBonay if he could pass across the stage. This was during the "dairy scene," which is set deep, leaving no room to cross behind the scenery. DeBonay crossed under the stage with Booth on the basement level. Then Booth exited the theatre and, through a passageway alongside, went out to 10th Street. He entered the Star Saloon and had a shot of whiskey.

About 10:00 p.m., after having looked into the lobby several times, he entered the theatre through one of the front doors. James E. Buckingham, the doorman, automatically extended his hand for a ticket. "You don't need a ticket, Buck,"[13] Booth replied. He then proceeded up the stairs to the dress circle (Buckingham remembered that he was humming a tune), well aware that the third act—his act—was under way. Booth's luck continued there. The guard who normally occupied the chair outside the alcove back of the boxes was not in place. Now he needed only to pass unnoticed through the outer door, secure it behind him with a bar, slip into Box 7, and wait.

Booth's moment was approaching. Dundreary was now alone on the stage, near the left exit, calling after Augusta and Mrs. Mountchessington (who had just insulted his manners):

> ' ... Don't know the manners of good society, eh? Wal, I guess I know enough to turn you inside out, old gal— you sockdologizing old man-trap. ... '

The audience responded predictably to the comeuppance given the two fortune hunters; even Mrs. Lincoln's laughter was observed—at the very instant that a sharp, pistol-like report was heard. Dropping the single shot deringer, Booth hissed in measured tones to the occupants of the box: "sic semper tyrannis" ("thus always to tyrants").[14] Major Rathbone was the first to grasp what had happened. He lunged for Booth, who deflected the attack with a long Bowie knife, stabbing Rathbone twice.

Still taking advantage of the surprise and bewilderment, Booth jumped the eleven feet from the box to the stage—his almost perfect escape foiled when he caught his spur in one of the Treasury Flags, which caused him to land unevenly and fracture the tibia of his right leg. Before crossing the stage to the right exit, he uttered the final words he would proclaim from the stage: "Revenge for the South!" He now crossed the stage—a distance of about forty feet—swept past Laura Keene, who was standing beside the prompter's box, and rushed down the broad right passageway to the rear door. On his way he passed orchestra leader William Withers who, annoyed over Miss Keene's decision to postpone "Honor to Our Soldiers" until the end of the performance, was standing in the passage on stage right. Booth slashed Withers twice. He then bolted out the door, kicked aside "Peanut" Burroughs, mounted, and rode off into the night.

The sequel to these events is well known. Panic reigned in the theatre as frantic efforts were made to save the President. Once the building was cleared, Lincoln was moved directly across 10th Street to the Petersen House, where he died the following morning at 7:22 a.m.

Booth, of course, fled immediately. His path carried him across the Navy Yard bridge and into Southern Maryland. Before being apprehended and shot on the morning of April 26 on the Garrett farm in Caroline County, Virginia (near Port Royal) he had crossed two broad rivers and spent many days hiding in the Maryland swamps. On July 7 four other individuals, convicted of conspiring with him, were hanged in Washington.

But long before this—well before the body of the slain President was laid to rest on May 4 in Springfield, Illinois—the enormity of the tragedy and its permanent effects had manifested themselves. In the generations that have followed the shadow of the tragedy has grown longer and darker, obscuring the lighthearted farce which added pleasure and humor to the last minutes of Lincoln's life.

What was the true nature of this play—its plot, its major characters, its themes? What was its stage history, both before and subsequent to the fated Washington performance? Who were the actors who shaped its success? Who, for that matter, was Tom Taylor, whose name occupies such an obscure niche in American history? These are but a few of the questions, the answers to which form a fascinating chronicle.

II

Tom Taylor (1817–1880), the son of a prosperous brewery executive, was born near Sunderland, on the northeast coast of England. After completing a B.A. (with honors) at Glasgow University and an M.A. at Cambridge, he tutored at Cambridge for two years before being named to a professorship in English literature at University College, London, in 1845. While performing his academic duties he read law at the Inner Temple, contributed to popular journals, and began writing for the stage. By the late 1840s his professional involvements included practising law, positions in public health and sanitation, art criticism (for the *Times* and the *Graphic*), biography, writing for the satirical magazine *Punch,* and playwriting.

The nineteenth century theatre for which Taylor wrote was characterized both in England and America by a multitude of dramatic forms—tragedies, histories, melodramas, farces, burlesques, dramatizations of popular fiction—many of which achieved contemporary success but are forgotten today. Nevertheless, most of Taylor's plays were popular on the stage, and his years as a playwright were pivotal ones for Victorian drama. His first efforts—*Cinderella,* a burlesque, and *A Trip to Kissingen,* a farce—were produced in 1844; his last, *Love or Life,* in 1878, two years before he died. Having begun his theatrical career at a rather low point in English drama, he ended it on the eve of a theatrical revival. Within two decades following his death in 1880, the British stage would be revitalized by such works as Henry Arthur Jones's *Saints and Sinners* (1884); Sir Arthur Wing Pinero's *The Profligate* (1889) and *The Second Mrs. Tanqueray* (1893); Oscar Wilde's *Lady Windermere's Fan* (1892) and *The Importance of Being Ernest* (1895); and George Bernard Shaw's *Arms and the Man* (1894) and *Caesar and Cleopatra* (1898).

Taylor's productivity (more than seventy-five plays in thirty-five years!) seems little short of amazing, given his other professional accomplishments. Still, his only play to achieve international fame and enduring celebrity (relatively speaking) was *Our American Cousin.* Moreover, as a scholar of his work has observed, even this distinction "was due only slightly to the work of its author and almost entirely to chance and to the performance of Edward Askew Sothern as Lord Dundreary."[15] It also seems ironic that Taylor's best-known play should have been written so early in his career (1851). However, irony informs much of the history of *Our American Cousin.*

III

Taylor seems to have gotten the idea for his play from the large number of Americans—an estimated 50,000—attending the Crystal Palace Exhibition in 1850–51.[16] Having a keen ear for unusual language and a reputation for incorporating it into drama, he was one of the many in his country to be captivated by the expressions of these colorful Yankee visitors. Judging from the Americanisms found in *Our American Cousin,* he was struck by the use of "guess" and "calculate" (for the more proper British "suppose"); personal epithets such as "old shoat" and "old hoss"; and droll colloquial verbs such as "make tracks" and "skedaddle."

Although seeing these "foreigners" at first hand was a novel experience for the English, it was also something of an anticlimax, for the Americans and their ways had been a favorite subject of travelling British authors for almost half a century. Between 1836 and 1860 alone some two hundred such books were published.[17] One of the most celebrated was by Mrs. Frances Trollope (mother of the Victorian novelist Anthony Trollope). Her *Domestic Manners of the Americans* (1832) went through four editions in the year of its appearance alone, and figured in debates on the first Reform Bill, which Parliament passed that year. Another popular example was Charles Dickens' *American Notes* (1842), based upon his observations during a much publicized tour of the United States. Both of these commentators painted a largely negative, and occasionally critical, picture of American life. Others were more positive, if perhaps not so sharply observant. Among them were Harriet Martineau, whose *Society in America* appeared in 1839, and Lady Emmeline Stuart Wortley, whose *Travels in the United States in 1849 and 1850* was published in 1851, during the Crystal Palace Exhibition. Mixed opinions notwithstanding, the British in 1851 were intensely curious about the distinctive character of this still evolving nation.[18]

Given the various Americans known to the English in the 1850s, one may logically ask which "type" Taylor intended in creating his "American cousin," Asa Trenchard. The Yankee was certainly prominent in his mind. Asa hails from Brattleboro, Vermont and exhibits certain traits of the stage prototype. He is plain of speech and at times awkward and unrefined in manner. Moreover, his bumpkin-like exterior belies a native shrewdness which is quick to penetrate sham and duplicity in certain of his cultural "superiors."[19] However, as Mrs. Mountchessington observes in Act II, Scene 1,

> ... We must study him. I think if you read up on Sam Slick a little, it might be useful, and just dip in to Bancroft's *History of the United States,* or some of Russell's *Letters;*[21] you should also know something of George Washington, of whom the Americans are justly proud.

In other words, Asa seems to have been intended to convey a general impression of an American, in a play representing national cultures rather than regions.

Taylor's protagonist may be short on refinement, but he is decidedly understanding and big-hearted. These traits are emphasized when he lights a cigar with the document entitling him to an English estate in order that Mary Meredith, who has been disinherited in his favor, may succeed to it. In depicting the extremes of cultural naivete and basic goodness in a single character, Tom Taylor unwittingly foreshadowed the "international" theme which later would be popularized in the work of Mark Twain, Henry James, and Edith Wharton. For example Asa's natural impulse to do the "right thing" by renouncing his legal rights can be compared with the actions of Henry James's Christopher Newman in *The American* (1877). This fictional protagonist of a later generation likewise commits to flames a document which would gain him personal benefits. Both in Taylor's play and in James's novel the selfless act is carried out in a European setting by one whose provincialism has been criticized by various members of a culture which, while ostensibly more "sophisticated," is apparently less vigorous and more corrupt. There is, however, an interesting difference in the two cases. Christopher Newman is the creation of a novelist born in the United States; Asa Trenchard, that of an English playwright. One is therefore impressed by Taylor's balanced treatment of the American character.

IV

It was for the American actor Joshua Silsbee, celebrated for his role in *The Forest Rose* and playing Yankee parts at the Adelphi Theatre in London in the early 1850s, that Taylor created the part of Asa. Upon completing the play, Taylor sold it (for 80 pounds) to a producer named Benjamin Webster late in 1851. By now the "Yankee mania" was subsiding, and Webster developed misgivings about producing it. So when Silsbee left England for America Webster gave him the script, along with the American rights. Silsbee carried it with him on tour, and even had it rehearsed. However, at the time of his death a few years later, it had not been acted.

Upon learning of Silsbee's death, Taylor asked John Chandler Bancroft Davis, a correspondent for the London *Times* in New York, to seek an American purchaser. Davis approached Lester Wallack, manager of a theatre on Broom Street in New York. Wallack took the play to Laura Keene, a popular actress, manager, playwright, and producer. He thought that Joseph Jefferson, who was then rehearsing for Keene's production of *A Midsummer Night's Dream,* might be ideal as Asa Trenchard. Keene was not immediately impressed but, on the advice of her business manager, John Lutz, she bought the play for $1,000. Shortly thereafter, her Shakespearean production was delayed by scene builders and painters, and she reconsidered *Our American Cousin* as a stop-gap production until her Shakespearean set was finished.

Thinking it a weak play and therefore in need of her best talent,[22] Keene turned to her Shakespearean company to cast the parts. For the lead she predictably chose Jefferson, who accepted. Casting the minor roles proved more difficult. The actor she chose for Binny, the butler, flatly refused. Another problem part was Lord Dundreary, for which she approached Edward Askew Sothern, a young English actor in the company. After reading the role, which consisted of only forty-seven lines, he declined. In desperation, she appealed again. Sothern's response, as later reported, was, " . . . If you will let me 'gag' [the part] and do what I please with it, I will undertake it, though it is pretty bad."[23] According to the same report, Keene replied, "Do anything you like with it, only play it."

The production of *Our American Cousin* which opened at Laura Keene's theatre on October 18, 1858 varied significantly from Taylor's original intentions. It was opening some seven years after the events which had occasioned its composition. It was being presented on a foreign stage—in the country, ironically, which had inspired its comic premise. Moreover, Taylor's script (which has not survived) was apparently a melodrama, a popular genre of the period. Melodrama generally features a romantic plot and exaggerated action, which appeals to emotions rather than to intellect. These elements are inherent in the basic situation of an American bumpkin in an English drawing room; in undoing the evils of a villainous lawyer; in the raucous drunken scene in the wine cellar; and in the happy-ever-after ending of paired lovers, righted wrongs, and solved problems. Such, however, was not the play which evolved from the initial production.

When Keene gave Sothern permission to "gag" the role of Lord Dundreary no one—least of all Sothern—could have foretold either the extent of his improvisations or the impact they would have on the play and its audiences. In his comprehensive study of Taylor's theatrical career, Winton Tolles has given a detailed account of these innovations:

> ... At first Jefferson was regarded as the stellar performer; but as the play ran on week after week Asa Trenchard became commonplace, and Lord Dundreary, with his well-bred air married to a vacant stare, his bland and hopeless stupidity mingled with an astonishing shrewdness, and his absurd mannerisms and inane lines, became the great attraction. As Sothern added 'gags' and 'business' [ad-lib performances], the part increased in prominence until it all but dwarfed the remainder of the play.

> The transformation of Lord Dundreary from a minor role in a mediocre drama into one of the most celebrated comic parts of the nineteenth century theatre was accomplished by a great character actor, not by accident, but by a conscious and shrewd attention to details of dress and manner, by the interpolation of numerous lines illuminating the eccentric and foolish character of the nobleman, and by studied and earnest effort. Sothern's make-up in the part was eccentric, but faultless and striking. In addition to the ankle-length coat, he adopted peg-top plaid trousers, a flowing cravat, long weeping whiskers, and a monocle. His speech was characterized by a quaint lisp and stutter ... In rewriting the part, Sothern introduced practically all the lines which, when accompanied by the perfectly expressed mannerisms, sent audiences into paroxysms of laughter. The twisted aphorisms known as 'Dundrearyisms', such as 'birds of a

15

feather gather no moss', created a vogue for this type of witticism. Equally popular were the absurd riddles which Dundreary continually propounded. Perhaps the most celebrated of Sothern's additions to the text was the letter from Dundreary's brother Sam, 'the immortal Sam who never had a 'uel'. The reading of this letter used to leave playgoers absolutely sore with laughter.[24]

T. Edgar Pemberton, Sothern's biographer, quotes a contemporary review which gives perhaps the most revealing analysis we have of Dundreary and his brand of humor.

> The type itself is new. It is the elaboration of a negation. Dundreary is an intellectual nonentity. It is as if the actor had set about to show us the rich fullness of a vacuum. But even a vacuum becomes eloquent when all the faculties of the artist are directed upon it ... Mr. Sothern conceived the idea of an elegant ass, perfect in all his imperfections, rich in the absence of brains, coherent in his incoherency, and polished in the proof of his stupidity. . . . [25]

As originally conceived, Dundreary had served as a minor farcical element in a melodrama. The expansion of that role resulted in the entire play taking on an aspect of farce, where action and dialogue are light and fanciful, and where conflicts do not threaten serious consequences. It is true that Sir Edward Trenchard is under siege from his creditors, but it is also obvious, early on, that the deviousness of Coyle, his nemesis, has been discovered by Asa, and that this rough-and-ready American has both the ability and the heart to set matters straight. Thus the building "crisis" can be discounted, as the primary focus becomes the zany verbal antics of Dundreary and the budding love between Asa and Mary Meredith.

The farcical aspect represents only one dimension of the play, however, and even after its expansion some of the original elements remained. One, described in Joseph Jefferson's *Autobiography*, offers particular insight into Taylor's original intentions:

> It was the opportunity of developing [the] attitude of early love, particularly love at first sight, that attracted me to the 'Cousin'. Simple and trifling as it looks, Mr.

Tom Taylor never drew a finer dramatic picture. The relation between the two characters was perfectly original. A shrewd, keen Yankee boy of twenty-five falls in love at first sight with a simple, loving, English dairymaid of eighteen. She sits innocently on the bench, close beside him; he is fascinated and draws closer to her; she raises her eyes in innocent wonder at this, and he glides gently to the farthest end of the bench. He never tells her of his love, nor does she in the faintest manner suggest her affection for him; and though they persistently talk of other things, you see plainly how deeply they are in love. . . .[26]

Originally scheduled for a two-week run, *Our American Cousin* ran for 140 nights. Audiences and reviewers were enthusiastic. Soon a production in German opened in New York at the the Stadt Theatre in the Bowery; it was but one of many subsequent continuations and adaptations. Even piracies of Keene's production began appearing. Her exclusive rights to the script having been challenged in a law suit[27] (which she won), her legal challengers—Wheatley and Clarke of the Arch Street Theatre in Philadelphia—sent stenographers to her performances. They took down the script in short hand, along with "every movement, every 'gag' "[28] and mounted their own production. Two Boston producers did the same.

The play was not produced immediately in England, however. Not until November 16, 1861 did a production open in London (at the Haymarket Theatre, with Sothern playing Dundreary). The initial response was disappointing. Had it not been for the urgings of Charles Mathews, a well known comic actor, it would have closed after a few performances. Then London audiences awoke suddenly to Dundreary's humor, and the play continued for more than 400 nights, a record for the London stage. Again its influence exceeded the theatre proper. English shops began doing a brisk business selling Dundreary shoes and other articles of clothing, as well as false whiskers and monocles. Pamphlets "dealing with the imaginary doings of Dundreary under every possible condition and in every quarter of the globe"[29] were said to be sold by the thousands on street corners. The shuffling gait which Sothern introduced into the role—based apparently upon dance steps in minstrel shows—was soon adopted as a popular dance known as the "Dundreary hop."

Sothern's influence did not stop there. In the absence of a copyright law forbidding such practices, he expanded the play to four acts and titled it *Dundreary.* He listed Taylor as the author, but noted that "The Character of Lord Dundreary [was] Written and Created by Mr. Sothern." He also wrote (sometimes with collaboration) shorter "after-pieces" such as "Dundreary Married and Settled" and "Dundreary a Father." Although he called them "wild whimsicalities,"[30] which were little more than burlesques of Taylor's original characters, they underscore the ongoing popularity of the role. He even wrote a comedy about Dundreary's brother Sam, titled *The Hon. Sam Slingsby,* which likewise attracted admirers.

V

The burgeoning Dundreary role was not the only change associated with *Our American Cousin.* In the words of Joseph Jefferson, "the success of the play proved the turning point in the career of three persons—Laura Keene, Sothern, and myself."[31] E. A. Sothern was to play Dundreary in both America and England until his retirement in 1880. Although he created other notable characterizations, in the public mind he remained Dundreary until the end. Starring in Keene's production led to Jefferson's taking the play, and his role, on tours of America and Australia. The role of Florence Trenchard was equally good for Laura Keene who, according to Jefferson, soon "began to twinkle with little brilliants [jewels]; gradually her splendor increased, until at the end of three months she was ablaze with diamonds."[32]

Although Keene apparently tired of the part before the end of the first season, she continued to play it until the end of her career. After terminating her management of the New York theatre in 1863, she toured much of the eastern United States during the remaning years of the Civil War, and it was these travels which brought to her to Washington in the spring of 1865. Her connections with *Our American Cousin* following the assassination appear somewhat equivocal. Although some accounts tell of her bravery in attending the wounded President, the trauma of the assassination was greater than she reckoned at the time. She did give the play many times during her remaining eight years of touring (she died in 1873); however, it was said that "she never made, or could bear to hear, the slightest allusion to that moment...."[33]

E. A. Sothern played Dundreary until the year before his death in 1881. Thereafter his son, E. H. Sothern, continued to act the role. He opened a four-act revival at the Lyric Theatre in New York on January 27, 1908.[34] Although this production met with luke-warm reviews, Sothern played the role as late as 1915. Thereafter the play became a kind of relic, seldom read and even less frequently performed.

John Wilkes Booth's use of the theatre, which he knew so well, to stage his own tragedy is one of history's bizarre ironies. But if the play was superseded by real life, it still offers modern readers an artistic creation rather than merely historical window-dressing. Critics should ask: Is its humor still fresh, its satire still poignant to generations far removed from its original audiences by time, social change, and technological advance? Can the vast numbers who travel to foreign countries today be interested in the dramatized confrontation of two cultures who find each other so strange? And can they laugh, as did their counterparts of a century and a quarter ago, at Dundreary's skewed witticisms?

The answer to these questions is "yes," for several reasons. First, altered though British and American cultures may be, each retains a sense of pride in its unique past. Second, despite their shared experiences during the twentieth century, considerable cultural differences remain. The play continues to remind the modern American reader of these distinctions, while reinforcing a sense of pride in the national character. Even a modern English reader stands to receive a certain sense of affirmation from *Our American Cousin*. For, despite initial expressions of cultural superiority, the English in the play are quick to recognize the generosity of the American visitor and to judge him on the basis of principles rather than manners. And finally, one may be gratified by a theatrical piece which, although farcical and exaggerated, and not nearly so lofty as the tragedy which overshadows it, reaffirms such timeless values as simple justice, understanding, and love.

And so, on this 125th anniversary of Abraham Lincoln's assassination, we offer *Our American Cousin* for reevaluation and appreciation. Ford's Theatre performed Phillips and Withers' "Honor to Our Soldiers" for the first time during the spring of 1990; now the play is available in a convenient and newly edited format. Perhaps the deepest irony is that the president who was best known and loved for his wit, who balanced America's darkest hour with optimism and humor, met his death in a moment of laughter; a moment that began the tragedy of Reconstruction and suffering that would persist for a century to come.

NOTES

1. Walt Whitman, "Death of Abraham Lincoln," *Prose Works* 1892, Vol. II, ed. Floyd Stovall. New York (1964), pp. 497–509.
2. Julia Adelaide Shepard, "Lincoln's Assassination Told by an Eye-Witness," *Century Magazine* 73(April, 1909), p. 918.
3. Ford's playbill of April 14, 1865.
4. Leonard Grover, "Lincoln's Interest in the Theatre," *Century Magazine* 73(April, 1909), p. 950. Tad, Lincoln's younger son, accompanied by his tutor, did attend the performance of *Aladdin* at Grover's that evening.
5. George S. Bryan, *The Great American Myth.* New York (1940), p. 150.
6. Bryan, p. 161.
7. *Ibid.,* p. 162.
8. It should be noted that numerous forgeries of the playbill appeared after the assassination. The best-known contains a statement that the performance would be "honored by the presence of President Lincoln." There are only two authentic states of the playbill: the first, the routine state printed early on the morning of the play date and the second, containing a stanza of "Honor to Our Soldiers," struck after the Presidential box was secured for the Lincoln party which, it was understood, would include General Grant. Neither of the authentic states contains a reference to Lincoln.
9. The musical number was never performed. Miss Keene delayed it twice, then decided that it would be presented at the conclusion of the performance, which of course was halted during Act III, Scene 2. Indeed, it was not performed until the spring of 1990.
10. William A. Tidwell, et al., *Come Retribution: The Confederate Secret Service and the Assassination of Lincoln.* Jackson & London (1988).
11. Jim Bishop, *The Day Lincoln Was Shot.* New York (1955), p. 130.
12. Shepard, p. 917.
13. Quoted in Bryan, p. 177.
14. Bishop, p. 210.
15. Winton Tolles, *Tom Taylor and the Victorian Drama.* New York (1940), p. 174.

16. It has been alleged that Taylor adapted his plot from a French play, *La Femme Fort* (1847).

17. Jules Zanger, ed. *Captain Frederick Marryat, 'Diary in America'*. Bloomington (1960), p. 28.

18. While Taylor correctly saw the influx of American tourists as a timely opportunity for an English comedy, American characters were no strangers on the nineteenth-century English stage. Nor, for that matter, was dramatizing American and British manners an original idea. Indeed, in Royall Tyler's *The Contrast* (1777), the first comedy written by an American, the action concerns differences between the two cultures. This play also introduced the Yankee, the earliest and perhaps most representative of all American character types. In the first half of the nineteenth century Yankees were featured in such American plays as Samuel Woodworth's *The Forest Rose, or American Farmers* (1825) and *Jonathan in England* (1828) (adapted from an earlier play by James H. Hackett, who later became one of Lincoln's favorite actors). These and other similar pieces became staples of American comedy, and some enjoyed success in England. For instance, after playing Jonathan Ploughboy in an American production of *The Forest Rose*, Joshua S. Silsbee (Some sources give the Christian name as "Joseph" or "Josiah" and the surname as "Silsby.") played it for more than 100 nights in London.

    Another American piece to win English acclaim was Harriet Beecher Stowe's novel *Uncle Tom's Cabin*. Tom Taylor and an English collaborator produced a dramatization titled *Slave Life* just weeks after this novel appeared in July, 1852. (It successfully premiered at the Adelphi Theatre in November of that year.) In 1865 *Rip Van Winkle*, newly adapted by Dion Boucicault, would become another exported classic. It was specifically written for the American actor Joseph Jefferson, who played it for 170 nights in London and thereafter for the remainder of his long and distinguished career.

19. Whitman (p. 504) states that Asa was "such a [Yankee] as was naver seen." However, it should be noted that Whitman makes light of the play in order to reinforce his depiction of the assassination as a grave and momentous event.

20. New York *Times*, October 19, 1858, p. 4.

21. Sam Slick: Yankee character featured in T. C. Haliburton's popular series of sketches, *The Clockmaker* (1837); George Bancroft (1800–1891): American statesman and scholar; Osborne Russell (1814–1865(?)): popular chronicler of the American Western frontier. References to buffalo, Indians, the prairie, etc. may derive from Russell.

22. Quoted in Tolles, p. 177.

23. *Ibid.*

24. *Ibid.,* pp. 178–79.

25. T. Edgar Pemberton, *A Memoir of Edward Askew Sothern.* London (1889), pp. 32–33.

26. Alan S. Downer, ed. *The Autobiography of Joseph Jefferson.* Cambridge, Mass. (1964), pp. 148–49.

27. See Pemberton, pp. 158–59 and "A Note on the Text" (below).

28. Pemberton, p. 159.

29. *Ibid.,* p. 31.

30. *Ibid.,* p. 58.

31. *Autobiography,* p. 147.

32. *Ibid.*

33. Quoted in John Creahan, *The Life of Laura Keene.* Philadelphia (1897), p. 65

34. There is even an irony in this revival. The production had tried out on December 12, 1907, in Washington, D.C. at the Belasco Theatre. This building was constructed on the site of the former home of Lincoln's Secretary of State, William H. Seward, who was savagely attacked there by Lewis Payne while the Lincolns attended the performance at Ford's.

A Note on the Text

Like many play texts of the nineteenth century and earlier, *Our American Cousin* exists in various states. The primary reason is that at this time there was no copyright protection to speak of. Fearing piracy, which was rampant in the early theatre, playwrights and owners of their work often did not publish plays. Thus, certain dramas which enjoyed contemporary fame and which are historically significant have been lost. [An excellent example is James K. Paulding's *Lion of the West,* which though well-known by reputation, was thought for more than a century to have disappeared completely. Only recently, has a script, published in 1954, been discovered in England.] In the absence of an "official" copyrighted text countless liberties were taken with scripts. Adaptations were freely made, and in them the creation of the original author was altered in all sorts of ways. Thus, many play texts existed in a fluid state, and the matter of determining a "pure" text—that reflecting the author's ultimate intentions: was, and remains, all but impossible.

Laura Keene, having paid $1,000 for *Our American Cousin,* guarded her property with care. However, sometime after the death of Joshua Silsbee his widow, finding among his papers the manuscript of the play bearing a notation ceding the play to her late husband, sold the script to two Philadelphia producers. These new owners, thinking that they had exclusive title to the property, took Miss Keene to court, but lost their suit. However, they blatantly sent stenographers to performances of Keene's production and pirated the script, which they subsequently produced. (Pemberton 158–59) This would explain why, at the time of its final performance at Ford's, it was announced that "[Keene] alone possesses the original manuscript, all other versions having been surreptitiously obtained and having but a faint resemblance to the original." (Bryan 176)

Keene did permit Joseph Jefferson to take the play on tour under a non-exclusive commission arrangement and in 1869, more than a decade after its initial performance, she allowed a version of the text to be printed, but carefully labelled it as "printed, but not published." This state, which George Bryan describes as "a wretchedly printed version from battered plates," (176) is but one of several surviving. Others exist in manuscript prompt books, which vary considerably among themselves and from the "printed, but not published" version of 1869. That text, for example, incorporates some of the expanded role of Dundreary, but does not include his show-stopping letter.

However, the more Sothern adapted, the more the text became a "Dundreary" play and the further it deviated from Taylor's original intentions. What follows, therefore, is an attempt to present a balanced text: one in which Dundreary is featured but does not dominate. As such, it aims at presenting the play in a rather advanced—as opposed to an extreme—state of evolution from the original. It is intended to approximate what an American audience might have seen when President Lincoln was part of that audience. For instance, it contains the lines ad-libbed in the final Ford's performance and mentioned above in the "Introduction." It also includes the full text of Dundreary's famous letter, a focal point of the stage productions. This is taken from Sothern's four-act adaptation, *Dundreary.*

Readers should observe certain caveats. Stage directions have been simplified in order that a clear mental image of placements and movements may be formed. When reading the Dundreary part it should be remembered that Sothern was by all accounts a master of comic timing. He cautioned that when lines were interrupted by laughter, "dead silence" should return before a speech was resumed. The letter reading was frequently interrupted; therefore, it could take a very long time to perform. The current edition includes his contingency directions for reading the various postscripts to the letter (Act III, Scene 4): they are optional, depending upon whether or not the laughter has begun to flag. Also, as his biographer noted, "one cannot on paper convey the comical stutter, the quaint laugh, and the wonderful facial expression of the actor [Sothern]." (Pemberton 41) Therefore, phonetic spelling for such mannerisms as lisps (e.g. "bwother" for "brother") is generally omitted. The reader must imagine such idiosyncrasies. However Binny's *H*s, preceding the initial vowels in certain words, have been included in order to indicate his Cockney origins.

The playwright Tom Taylor (seated center) dressed for a role in a theatrical benefit circa 1867.

Laura Keene as Florence Trenchard.

Joseph Jefferson as Asa Trenchard, the "American Cousin"

Edward A. Sothern as Lord Dundreary

The playbill announcing the April 14, 1865 performance of *Our American Cousin*. This is the authentic second state, containing a stanza of H. B. Phillips' "Honor to Our Soldiers."

A Woodcut of Ford's Theatre as it appeared in Lincoln's day. The original structure had been the site of the First Baptist Church until 1859. John T. Ford bought the building and turned it into a theatre in 1861, then replaced it with this new structure in 1863. To the right is the tavern where Booth waited for the third act to begin.

On April 14, 1865 a weary Lincoln nearly cancelled his evening at the theatre. But after General Grant declined Lincoln's invitation to attend, the President did not want to disappoint an expectant public. This was the final photograph of Lincoln, taken on April 9, 1865, the day of Lee's surrender to Grant and five days before the assassination.

John Wilkes Booth. An actor himself, Booth was no stranger to Ford's Theatre, and gained easy entrance to the Presidential box the night of the assassination.

After fatally shooting the President, Booth leaped from the Presidential box to the stage, but caught his spur on the flag, as shown in this illustration from *Frank Leslie's Weekly.*

This diagram of Ford's shows how Booth was able to make his escape. After leaping from the Presidential box (above i) to the left of the stage, he then crossed the stage, limping from the broken leg he sustained in the fall, and along passageway (r) and out the rear door (s) to a horse he had waiting for him in the back alley (u).

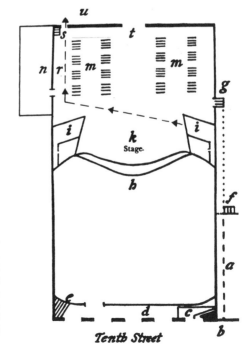

Tenth Street

The President, mortally wounded, was taken to the Peterson house across the street from the theatre. This is a drawing of the deathbed scene by John Littlefield. Lincoln died April 15, 1865 at 7:22 a.m.

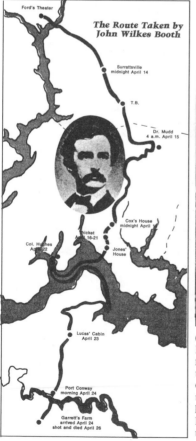

The Route Taken by John Wilkes Booth

Ford's Theater

Surrattsville
midnight April 14

T.B.

Dr. Mudd
4 a.m. April 15

Cox's House
midnight April

Thicket
April 16-21

Col. Hughes
April 22

Jones'
House

Lucas' Cabin
April 23

Port Conway
morning April 24

Garrett's Farm
arrived April 24
shot and died April 26

(Above) Ford's Theatre is draped in black following the assassination. The billboard in the foreground announces *The Octoroon,* the play that was scheduled for the evening following *Our American Cousin.* (Left) The escape route taken by Booth. Ten days after the assassination, he was fatally shot at Garrett's farm in Virginia. Four of his conspirators were subsequently tried and hanged.

OUR AMERICAN COUSIN

CAST OF CHARACTERS

LORD DUNDREARY: a guest at Trenchard Manor

ASA TRENCHARD: the Trenchards' "American cousin"

SIR EDWARD TRENCHARD: Lord of Trenchard Manor

CAPTAIN DE BOOTS: suitor of Augusta

LT. HARRY VERNON, R.N.: suitor of Florence

ABEL MURCOTT: clerk to Coyle

MR. COYLE: an attorney

BUDDICOMBE: valet to Lord Dundreary

BINNY: butler to Sir Edward

JOHN WICKENS: a gardener

MRS. MOUNTCHESSINGTON: a guest at Trenchard Manor

FLORENCE TRENCHARD: daughter of Sir Edward

MARY MEREDITH: niece of Sir Edward

AUGUSTA: daughter of Mrs. Mountchessington

GEORGINA: daughter of Mrs. Mountchessington

SHARPE: a house maid

SKILLET: a scullery servant

ACT ONE

Scene 1

Foreground is the drawing room of Trenchard Manor; the backdrop features a large French window through which a fine English park is seen; right is an interior dining room with luncheon spread; left is an open archway with a balcony behind. A table, right forward, is spread with books, papers, and a work basket containing wools and an embroidery frame; left. forward are a fashionable arm chair and sofa; a small table is near the center. Stage handsomely set, costly furniture, carpet down, chairs, etc.

BUDDICOMBE discovered on sofa reading newspaper. SKILLET and SHARPE busily arranging furniture as curtain rises.

SHARPE: I don't know how you may feel as a visitor, Mr. Buddicombe, but I think this is a most uncomfortable family.

BUDDICOMBE: Very uncomfortable. I have no curtain to my bed.

SKILLET: And no wine at the second table.

SHARPE: And meaner servants I never seed.

BUDDICOMBE: I'm afraid Sir Edward is in a queer strait. He cannot be in as good circumstances as he was. Why, there has not been a new carpet on the parlor floor for a month.

SKILLET: Yes, for only this morning I was speaking to Mr. Binny. 'Mrs. Skillet,' says he—

Enter BINNY, left.

BINNY: Mind your hown business instead hof your betters. I'm disgusted with you lower servants. When the wine merchant presents his bills, you men, hear me, don't say he's been pressing for the last six months, do you?

SKILLET: Nor I, that the last year's milliner's bills have not been paid.

SHARPE: Nor I, that Miss Florence has not had no new dresses from London all winter.

BUDDICOMBE: And I can solemnly swear that his lordship's hair has been faithfully bound in his bosom.

BINNY: That'll do, that'll do; but to remember to check hidle curiosity is the first duty of men hin livery. Ha, 'ere we have the letters.

Enter JOHN WICKENS, left, with green baize bag. BINNY takes bag, takes out letters and reads addresses.

BINNY: Hah! Bill, of course, Miss Augusta, Mrs. Mountchessington, Lord Dundreary . . . Capt. de Boots . . . Miss Georgina Mountchessington . . . Lieut. Vernon . . . Ah! That's from the Admiralty. What's this? Miss Florence Trenchard. via Brattleboro', V-e-r-m-o-n-t . . .

BUDDICOMBE: Where's that, Mr. Binney?

WICKENS: Why, that be hin the United States of North Hamerica, and a main good place for poor folks.

BINNY: John Wickens, you forget yourself.

WICKENS: Beg pardon, Mr. Binny.

BINNY: John Wickens, leave the room.

WICKENS: But I know where Vermont be, tho'.

BINNY: John Wickens, get hout. *[Exit WICKENS, left]*

BUDDICOMBE: Dreadful fellow, that.

BINNY: Halways himpudent.

BUDDICOMBE *[Looking at letter in BINNY's hand]*:   Why, that is Sir Edward's hand, Mr. Binny, he must have been sporting.

BINNY: Yes, shooting wild helephants and buffalos what abound there.

BUDDICOMBE: The nasty beasts. *[Looking off right]* Hello. Here comes Miss Florence tearing across the lane like a three year old colt.

SHARP, SKILLET *[Together]*:   Oh, Gemini. *[Run off right; BUDDICOMBE runs off, left]*

Enter FLORENCE, right.

FLORENCE *[As if after running]*:   Oh! I'm fairly out of breath. Good morning, Binny, the letter bag I saw coming, Wickens coming with it. I thought I could catch him before I reached the house. *[Sits, right]* So off I started. I forgot the pond—it was in or over. I got over, but my hat got in. *[To BINNY]* I wish you'd fish it out for me; you won't find the pond very deep.

BINNY: Me fish for an 'at? Does she take me for an hangler? 'Orrid!

FLORENCE: Give me the letters. *[Takes them]* Ah, blessed budget that descends upon Trenchard Manor, like rain on a duck pond. Tell Papa and all that the letters have come. You will find them on the terrace.

BINNY: Yes, Miss. *[Going, left]*

FLORENCE: And then go fish my hat out of the pond, it's not very deep.

BINNY *[Aside]:* Me fish for 'ats? I wonder if she takes me for an hangler? *[Exit right, disgusted]*

FLORENCE *[Reading directions]:* Lieutenant Vernon. *[This is a large letter with a large white envelope, red seal]* In Her Majesty's service. Admiralty. R.N. Ah, that's the answer to Harry's application for a ship. Papa promised to use his influence for him. I hope he has succeeded, but then he will have to leave us, and who knows if he ever comes back. What a foolish girl I am, when I know that his rise in the service will depend upon it. I do hope he'll get it, and, if he must leave us, I'll bid him good-bye as a lass who loves a sailor should.

Enter SIR EDWARD, MRS. MOUNTCHESSINGTON, AUGUSTA, CAPT. DE BOOTS, VERNON, *left.*

FLORENCE: Papa, dear, here are letters for you, one for you, Mrs. Mountchessington, one for you, Capt. de Boots, and one for you, Harry. *[Hiding the Vermont letter behind her]*

VERNON: One for me, Florence? Ah, I know you have from the roguish twinkle of your eyes.

FLORENCE: Now what will you give me for one?

VERNON: Ah, then you have one?

FLORENCE: Yes, there, Harry. *[Gives it]*

VERNON: Ah, for a ship. *[Opens and reads]*

FLORENCE: Ah! *Mon ami,* you are to leave us. Good news, or bad?

VERNON: No ship yet; this promises another year of land lubbery *[Goes up]*

FLORENCE: I'm so sorry. *[Aside]* I'm so glad he's not going away. But where's Dundreary? Has anybody seen Dundreary?

Enter DUNDREARY.

DUNDREARY: Good morning, Mith Florence.

FLORENCE *[Comes down, left]:* Good morning, my Lord Dundreary. Who do you think has been here. What does the postman bring?

DUNDREARY: Well, sometimes he brings a bag with a lock on it, sometimes newspapers, and sometimes letters, I suppothe.

FLORENCE: There. *[Gives letter. DUNDREARY opens letter and FLORENCE goes up right. DUNDREARY knocks knees against chair, turns round, knocks shins, and at last is seated at extreme right]*

DUNDREARY: Thank you. *[Reads letter]*

DE BOOTS *[Reading letter]*:   By Jove, old Soloman has made a crop of it.

DUNDREARY: A—what of it?

DE BOOTS: Beg pardon, an event I'm deeply interested in, that's all. I beg pardon.

AUGUSTA: Ah! Florence, dear, there's a letter of yours got among mine. *[Gives it]*

FLORENCE: Why Papa, it's from dear brother Ned.

SIR EDWARD: From my boy! Where is he? How is he? Read it.

FLORENCE: He writes from Brattleboro', Vermont. *[Reads letter]* 'Quite well, just come in from a shooting excursion, with a party of Crows, splendid fellows, six feet high'.

DUNDREARY: Birds six feet high, what tremendous animals they must be.

FLORENCE: Oh, I see what my brother means; a tribe of Indians called Crows, not birds.[1]

DUNDREARY: Oh, I thought you meant those creatures with wigs on them.

FLORENCE: Wigs!

DUNDREARY: I mean those things that move, breathe and walk, they look like animals with those things. *[Moving his arms like wings]*

FLORENCE: Wings.

DUNDREARY: Birds with wings. That's the idea.

FLORENCE *[Still reading letter]*:   'Bye-the-bye, I have lately come quite hap-hazard upon the other branch of our family, which emigrated to America at the Restoration. They are now thriving in this State, and discovering our relationship, they received me

---

1. Placing this tribe of plains Indians in Vermont was one of the geographical lapses for which Taylor was criticized.

most hospitably. I have cleared up the mysterious death of old Mark Trenchard'.

SIR EDWARD: Of my uncle?

FLORENCE *[Reading letter]:*   'It appears that when he quarreled with his daughter on her marriage with poor Meredith, he came here in search of his stray shoot of the family tree, found them and died in their house, leaving Asa, one of the sons, heir to his personal property in England, which ought to belong to poor Mary Meredith. Asa is about to sail for the old country to take possession. I gave him directions to find you out, and he should arrive almost as soon as this letter. Receive him kindly for the sake of the kindness he has shown to me, and let him see some of our shooting'. Your affectionate brother, NED.

SIR EDWARD: An American branch of the family.

MRS. MOUNT: Oh, how interesting!

AUGUSTA *[Enthusiastically]:*   How delightfully romantic! I can imagine the wild young hunter. An Apollo of the prairie...

FLORENCE: An Apollo of the prairie; yes, with a strong nasal twang, and a decided taste for tobacco and cobblers.

SIR EDWARD: Florence, you forget that he is a Trenchard, and no true Trenchard would have a liking for cobblers or low people of that kind.

FLORENCE: I hate him, whatever he is, coming here to rob poor cousin Mary of her grandmother's guineas.

SIR EDWARD: Florence, how often must I request you not to call Mary Meredith your cousin?

FLORENCE: Why, she is my cousin, is she not? Besides she presides over her milk pail like a duchess playing dairy maid. *[SIR EDWARD goes up]* Ah! Papa won't hear me speak of my poor cousin, and then I'm so fond of syllabubs. Dundreary, do you know what syllabubs are?

DUNDREARY: Oh, yeth. I know what a syllabub is—yeth—yeth.

FLORENCE: Why, I don't believe you do know what they are.

DUNDREARY: Not know what syllabubs are? That's a good idea. Why they are—they are—only babies, idiotic children; that's a good idea, that's good. *[Bumps head against FLORENCE]*

FLORENCE: No, it's not a bit like the idea. What you mean are called cherubims.

DUNDREARY: What, those things that look like oranges, with wings on them?

FLORENCE: Not a bit like it. Well, after luncheon you must go with me and I'll introduce you to my cousin Mary and syllabubs.

DUNDREARY: I never saw Mr. Syllabubs, I am sure.

FLORENCE: Well, now, don't forget.

DUNDREARY: I can never forget—when I can recollect.

FLORENCE: Then recollect that you have an appointment with me after luncheon.

DUNDREARY: Yeth, yeth.

FLORENCE: Well, what have you after luncheon?

DUNDREARY: Well, sometimes I have a glass of brandy with an egg in it, sometimes a run 'round the duck pond, sometimes a game of checkers—that's for exercise—and perhaps a game of billiards.

FLORENCE: No, no; you have with me after luncheon, an ap— an ap—

DUNDREARY: An ap— an ap—

FLORENCE: An ap— an appoint—appointment.

DUNDREARY: An ointment, that's the idea. *[Knocks against* DE BOOTS *as they go upstage]*

MRS. MOUNT *[Aside]:*   That artful girl has designs upon Lord Dundreary. Augusta, dear, go see how your poor, dear sister is this morning.

AUGUSTA: Yes, mamma. *[Exit, left]*

MRS. MOUNT: She is a great sufferer, my dear.

DUNDREARY: Yeth, but a lonely one.

FLORENCE: What kind of night had she?

MRS. MOUNT: Oh, a very refreshing one, thanks to the draught you were kind enough to prescribe for her, Lord Dundreary.

FLORENCE: What! Has Lord Dundreary been prescribing for Georgina?

DUNDREARY: Yeth. You see I gave her a draught that cured the effect of the draught, and that draught was a draft that didn't pay the doctor's bill. Didn't that draught—

FLORENCE: Good gracious! What a number of draughts. You have almost a game of draughts.

DUNDREARY: Ha! Ha! Ha!

FLORENCE: What's the matter?

DUNDREARY: That wath a joke, that wath.

FLORENCE: Where's the joke? *[DUNDREARY screams and turns to Mrs. MOUNTCHESSINGTON]*

MRS. MOUNT: No.

DUNDREARY: She don't see it—

{FLORENCE *[Suddenly interrupting]*: Anybody can see *that!*}[2]

DUNDREARY: ... Don't you see—a game of dwafts—pieces of wound wood on square pieces of leather. That's the idea. Now, I want to put your brains to the test. I want to ask you a whime?

FLORENCE: A whime? What's that?

DUNDREARY: A whime is a widdle, you know.

FLORENCE: A widdle!

DUNDREARY: Yeth; one of those things, like—why is so and so or somebody like somebody else.

FLORENCE: Oh, I see, you mean a conundrum.

DUNDREARY: Yeth, a drum, that's the idea. What is it gives a cold in the head, cures a cold, pays the doctor's bill and makes the home-guard look for substitutes. *[FLORENCE repeats it]* Yeth. Do you give up?

FLORENCE: Yes.

DUNDREARY: Well, I'll tell you—a draught. Now, I've got a better one than that: When is a dog's tail not a dog's tail?

FLORENCE *[Repeats. During this FLORENCE, MRS. MOUNTCHESSINGTON, and DUNDREARY are downstage]*

DUNDREARY: Yeth, that's a stunner. You've got to give that up.

FLORENCE: Yes, and willingly.

DUNDREARY: When it's a cart. *[They look at him inquiringly]*

FLORENCE: Why, what on earth does a dog's tail have to do with a cart?

DUNDREARY: When it moves about, you know. A horse makes a cart move, so does a dog make his tail move.

FLORENCE: Oh, I see what you mean—when it's a *wag*-on. *[Wags the letter in her hand]*

---

2. This line was ad-libbed by Laura Keene in the April 14, 1865 performance to indicate the arrival of the Lincoln party.

DUNDREARY: Well, a wagon and a cart are the same thing, ain't they? That's the idea—it's the same thing.

FLORENCE: They are not the same. In the case of your conundrum there's a very great difference.

DUNDREARY: Now I've got another. Why does a dog waggle his tail?

FLORENCE: Upon my word, I never inquired.

DUNDREARY: Because the tail can't waggle the dog. Ha! Ha!

FLORENCE: Ha! Ha! Is that your own, Dundreary?

DUNDREARY: Now I've got one, and this one is original.

FLORENCE: No, no, don't spoil the last one.

DUNDREARY: Yeth; but this one is extremely interesting.

MRS. MOUNT: Do you think so, Lord Dundreary?

DUNDREARY: Yeth. Miss Georgina likes me to tell her my jokes. Bye-the-bye, talking of that lovely sufferer, isn't she an interesting invalid? They do say that's what the matter with me. I'm an interesting invalid.

FLORENCE: Oh, that accounts for what I have heard so many young ladies say—Florence, dear, don't you think Lord Dundreary's extremely interesting? I never knew what they meant before.

DUNDREARY: Yeth, the doctor recommends me to drink donkey's milk.

FLORENCE *[Hiding laugh]*:   Oh, what a clever man he must be. He knows we generally thrive best on our native food. *[Goes up]*

DUNDREARY *[Looking first at* FLORENCE *and then at* MRS. MOUNTCHESSINGTON]*:   I'm so weak, and that is so strong. Yes, I'm naturally very weak, and I want strengthening. Yes, I'll try it.

Enter AUGUSTA. *Business with* DUNDREARY, *who finally exits and brings on* GEORGINA, *left.*

DUNDREARY: Look at this lonely sufferer. *[Bringing on* GEORGINA, *seats her on sofa, left]* There, repothe yourself.

GEORGINA *[Fanning herself]*:   Thank you, my lord. Everybody is kind to me, and I am so delicate.

AUGUSTA *[At table]*:   Capt. de Boots, do unravel these wools for me, you have such an eye for color.

FLORENCE: An eye for color! Yes, especially green.

DUNDREARY *[Screams]*:   Ha! Ha! Ha!

ALL: What's the matter?

DUNDREARY: Why, that wath a joke, that wath.

FLORENCE: Where was the joke?

DUNDREARY: Especially, ha! Ha!

SIR EDWARD: Florence, dear, I must leave you to represent me to my guests. These letters will give me a great deal of business to-day.

FLORENCE: Well, Papa, remember that I am your little clerk and person of all work.

SIR EDWARD: No, no; this is private business—money matters, my love, which women know nothing about. *[Aside]* Luckily for them. I expect Mr. Coyle to-day.

FLORENCE: Dear papa, how I wish you would get another agent.

SIR EDWARD: Nonsense, Florence, impossible. He knows my affairs. His father was agent for the late Baronet. He is one of the family, almost.

FLORENCE: Papa, I have implicit faith in my own judgment of faces. Depend upon it, that man is not to be trusted.

SIR EDWARD: Florence, you are ridiculous. I could not get on a week without him. *[Aside]* Curse him, I wish I could! Coyle is a most intelligent agent, and a most faithful servant of the family.

Enter BINNY, left.

BINNY: Mr. Coyle and hagent with papers.

SIR EDWARD: Show him into the library. I will be with him presently. *[Exit BINNY]*

FLORENCE: Father, I thought you promised me you would get rid of that Mr. Coyle.

SIR EDWARD *[Aside]:* Curse him, I wish I could! *[To FLORENCE]* But Florence, Mr. Coyle has been in the family a great many years. His father was with my father. Now good-bye.

FLORENCE: Remember the archery meeting, Papa. It is at three.

SIR EDWARD: Yes, yes, I'll remember. *[Aside]* Pretty time for such levity when ruin stares me in the face. Florence, I leave you as my representative. *[Aside]* Now to prepare myself to meet my Shylock. *[Exit, right]*

FLORENCE: Why will Papa not trust me? *[VERNON comes down, right]* Oh, Harry! I wish he would find out what a lot of pluck and common sense there is in this feather head of mine.

DUNDREARY: Miss Florence, will you be kind anough to tell Miss Georgina all about that American relative of yours?

FLORENCE: Oh, about my American cousin; certainly. *[Aside to VERNON]* Lets have some fun. Well, he's about 17 feet high.

DUNDREARY: Good gracious! 17 feet high!

FLORENCE: They are all 17 feet high in America, ain't they, Mr. Vernon?

VERNON: Yes, that's about the average height.

FLORENCE: And they have long black hair that reaches down to their heels; they have dark copper-colored skin, and they fight with—what do they fight with, Mr. Vernon?

VERNON: Tomahawks and scalping knives.

FLORENCE: Yes, and you'd better take care, Miss Georgina, or he'll take his tomahawk and scalping knife and scalp you immediately.

GEORGINA screams and faints.

DUNDREARY: Here, somebody get something and throw over her; a pail of water; no, not that, she's pale enough already. *[Fans her with handkerchief]* Georgina, don't be afraid. Dundreary's by your side. He will protect you.

FLORENCE: Don't be frightened, Georgina. He will never harm you while Dundreary is about. Why, he could get three scalps here.

Pulls DUNDREARY's whiskers. GEORGINA screams.

DUNDREARY: Don't scream. I won't lose my whiskers. I know what I'll do for my own safety. I will take this handkerchief and tie the roof of my head on. *[Ties it on]*

FLORENCE *[Pretending to cry]*:   Good-bye, Dundreary. I'll never see you again in all your glory.

DUNDREARY: Don't cry, Miss Florence. I'm ready for Mr. Tommy Hawk.

Enter BINNY.

BINNY: If you please, Miss, 'ere's a gent what says he's hexpected.

FLORENCE: What's his name? Where's his card?

BINNY: He didn't tell me his name, Miss, and when I haxed him for his card 'e said 'e had a whole pack in his valise, and if I 'ad a mine 'e'd play me a game of seven hup. He says he has come to stay, and he certainly looks as if he didn't mean to go.

FLORENCE: That's him. Show him in, Mr. Binny. *[Exit BINNY, left]* That's my American cousin, I know.

AUGUSTA *[Romantically]:* Your American cousin! Oh, how delightfully romantic, isn't it, Capt. de Boots? *[Comes down]* I can imagine the wild young hunter, with the free step and the majestic mien of the hunter of the forest.

ASA *[Outside, left]:* Consarn your picture, didn't I tell you I was expected? You are as obstinate as Deacon Stumps' forelock, that wouldn't lie down and couldn't stand up. Wouldn't pint forward and couldn't go backward.

Enter ASA, left, carrying a valise. Servants appear in door, laughing. FLORENCE waves them back.

ASA: Where's the squire?

FLORENCE: Do you mean Sir Edward Trenchard, sir?

ASA: Yes.

FLORENCE: He is not present, but I am his daughter.

ASA: Well, I guess that'll fit about as well if you tell this darned old shoat to take me to my room.

FLORENCE: What does he mean by "shoat"?

BINNY *[Taking valise]:* He means me, Mum; but what he wants—

ASA: Hurry up, old hoss!

BINNY: He calls me a 'oss, Miss, I suppose I shall be a hox next, or perhaps an 'ogg.

ASA: Wal, darn me, if you ain't the consarnedest old shoat I ever did see since I was baptized Asa Trenchard.

FLORENCE: Ah! Then it is our American cousin. Glad to see you— my brother told us to expect you.

ASA: Wal, yes, I guess you do b'long to my family. I'm Asa Trenchard, born in old Vermont, suckled on the banks of Muddy Creek, about the tallest gunner, the fastest runner, the slickest dancer, and generally the loudest critter in the state. You're my cousin, be you? Wal, I ain't got no objections to kiss you, as one cousin ought to kiss another.

VERNON: Sir, how dare you?

ASA: Are you one of the family? Cause if you ain't, you've got no right to interfere, and if you be, you needn't be alarmed: I ain't going to kiss you. Here's your young man's letter. *[Gives letter and attempts to kiss her]*

45

FLORENCE: In the old country, Mr. Trenchard, cousins content themselves with hands, but our hearts are with them. You're welcome; there is mine. *[Gives her hand, which he shakes heartily]*

ASA: That'll do about as well. I won't kiss you if you don't want me to; but if you did, I wouldn't stop on account of that sailor man.

VERNON *[Makes threatening gesture at ASA]:* Sir!

ASA: Hold your horses! Now you needn't get your back up. What an all-fired huffy chap you are. *[To FLORENCE]* Now if you'll have this old hoss show me to my room, I should like to fix up a bit and put on a clean buzzom. *[All start]* Why, what on earth is the matter with you all? I only spoke because you're so all-fired go-to-meetin' like.

FLORENCE: Show Mr. Trenchard to the red room, Mr. Binny, that is if you're done with it, Lord Dundreary.

DUNDREARY: Yeth, Miss Florence. The room and I have got through with each other, yeth.

ASA and DUNDREARY see each other for the first time. Business of recognition, ad lib.

ASA: Concentrated essence of baboons, what on earth is that?

FLORENCE: Oh, pray excuse me. Permit me to introduce you to my American cousin, Asa Trenchard, Lord Dundreary.

ASA *[Extends his hand]:* Give me a shake of your hand' like a man. *[Business of shaking hands]*

DUNDREARY: If you call that shaking hands like a man I call it shaking hands like a steam engine. I declare, you've shaken all the brains in my head. *[Aside]:* He's mad. Yes, Miss Florence, I've done with that room. *[Aside]* He's racked my brain.

ASA: You don't mean to say that you've got any brains.

DUNDREARY: No, sir, such a thing never entered my head. You want to find out if I've got any brains so the wed Indians can scalp me. *[Holding hands to his head]*

FLORENCE: The red room, then, Mr. Binny.

ASA *[To BINNY]:* Hold on! *[Examines him]* Wal, darn me, but you keep your help in all-fired good order here. *[Feels of him]* This old shoat is fat enough to kill. *[Hits BINNY in the stomach. BINNY runs off, left]* Mind how you go up stairs, old hoss, or you'll bust your biler. *[Exit, left]*

DUNDREARY: Now he thinks Binny's an engine, and has got a boiler.

FLORENCE: Oh, what fun!

AUGUSTA: I'm so glad he has gone. He frightened me very much. What a strange creature! He's not very romantic.

FLORENCE: Ah, where's your young hunter? Your Apollo of the prairie? *[Laughs]*

MRS. MOUNT: Old Mark Trenchard died very rich, did he not, Florence?

FLORENCE: Very rich, I believe,.

AUGUSTA: He's not at all romantic, is he, Mamma?

MRS. MOUNT *[Aside to her]*:   My dear, I have no doubt he has solid good qualities, and I don't want you to laugh at him like Florence Trenchard.

AUGUSTA: No, mamma, I won't.

FLORENCE: But what are we to do with him?

DUNDREARY: Ha! Ha! Ha!

ALL: What's the matter?

DUNDREARY: I've got an idea.

FLORENCE: Oh! Let's hear Dundreary's idea.

DUNDREARY: It's so seldom that I get an idea that when I do get one it startles me. Let us get a pickle bottle.

FLORENCE: Pickle bottle! *[All come down]*

DUNDREARY: Yeth; one of those things with glass sides.

Enter ASA, left.

FLORENCE: Oh! You mean a glass case.

DUNDREARY: Yeth, a glass case, that's the idea, and let us put this Mr. Thomas Hawk in it, and have him on exhibition. That's the idea.

ASA *[Down left of FLORENCE, overhearing]*:   Oh! That's your idea, is it? Wal, stranger, I don't know what they're going to do with me, but wherever they do put me, I hope it will be out of the reach of a jackass. I'm a real hoss, I am, and I get kinder riley with those critters.

DUNDREARY: Now he thinks he's a horse. I've heard of a great jackass, and I dreampt of a jackass, but I don't believe there is any such insect.

FLORENCE: Well, cousin, I hope you made yourself comfortable.

ASA: Well, no, I can't say as I did. You see there was so many all-fired fixin's in my room I couldn't find anything I wanted.

FLORENCE: What was it you couldn't find in your room?

ASA: There was no soft soap.

DE BOOTS: Soft soap!

AUGUSTA: Soft soap!

VERNON: Soft soap!

MRS. MOUNT: Soft soap!

FLORENCE: Soft soap!

GEORGINA [*On sofa*]: Soft soap!

DUNDREARY: Thoft thoap!

ASA: Yes, soft soap. I reckon you know what that is. However, I struck a pump in the kitchen, slicked my hair down a little, gave my boots a lick of grease, and now I feel quite handsome; but I'm everlastingly dry.

FLORENCE: You'll find ale, wine and luncheon on the side table.

ASA: Wal, I don't know as I've got any appetite. You see comin' along on the cars I worried down half a dozen ham sandwiches, eight or ten boiled eggs, two or three pumpkin pies and a string of cold sausages—and—wal, I guess I can hold on till dinner time.

DUNDREARY: Did that illustrious exile eat all that? I wonder where he put it.

ASA: I'm as dry as a sap tree in August.

BINNY [*Throwing open inner door*]: Luncheon!

ASA [*Goes hastily to the table*]: Wal, I don't want to speak out too plain, but this is an awful mean set out for a big house like this.

FLORENCE: Why, what's wrong, sir?

ASA: Why, there's no mush.

DUNDREARY: No mush?

ASA: Nary slapjack.

DUNDREARY: Why does he want to slap Jack?

ASA: No pork and beans.

DUNDREARY: Pork's been here, but he's left.

ASA: And where on airth's the clam chowder?

DUNDREARY: Where *is* clam chowder? He's never here when he's wanted.

Asa [*Drinks and spits*]: Here's your health, old hoss. Do you call that a drink? See here, cousin, you seem to be the liveliest critter here, so just hurry up the fixin's, and I'll show the benighted aristocratic society what real liquor is. So hurry up the fixin's.

ALL: Fixin's?

FLORENCE: What do you mean by fixin's?

Asa: Why, brandy, rum, gin and whisky. We'll make them all useful.

FLORENCE: Oh, I'll hurry up the fixin's. What fun! [*Exit, right*]

DUNDREARY: Oh! I thought he meant the gas fixins.

Asa [*To BINNY*]: Say, you, Mr. Puffy, you run out and get me a bunch of mint and a bundle of straws; hurry up, old hoss. [*Exit BINNY, left, indignantly*] Say, Mr. Sailor man, just help me down with this table. Oh! Don't you get riley, you and I ran against each other when I came in, but we'll be friends yet. [*VERNON helps him with table to center*]

Enter FLORENCE, followed by servants in livery; they carry a case of decanters and water, on which are seven or eight glasses, two or three tin mixers and a bowl of sugar. BINNY enters with a bunch of mint and a few straws.

FLORENCE: Here, cousin, are the fixin's.

Asa: That's yer sort. Now then, I'll give you all a drink that'll make you squeal. [*To BINNY*] Here, Puffy, just shake that up, faster. I'll give that sick gal a drink that'll make her squirm like an eel on a mudbank.

DUNDREARY [*Screams*]: What an horrible idea. [*Runs about stage*]

FLORENCE: Oh, don't mind him! That's only an American joke.

DUNDREARY: A joke! Do you call that a joke? To make a sick girl squirm like a mud bank on an eel's skin?

Asa: Yes, I'll give you a drink that'll make your whiskers return under your chin, which is their natural location. Now, ladies and gentlemen, what'll you have, Whisky Skin, Brandy Smash, Sherry Cobbler, Mint Julep or Jersey Lightning?

AUGUSTA: Oh, I want a mint julep.

DE BOOTS: Give me a Gin Cocktail.

FLORENCE: I'll take a Sherry Cobbler.

VERNON: Brandy Smash for me.

MRS. MOUNT: Give me a Whisky Skin.

GEORGINA: I'll take a Lemonade.

DUNDREARY: Give me a Jersey Lightning.

ASA: Give him a Jersey Lightning. *[As DUNDREARY drinks]* Warranted to kill a forty rods. *[DUNDREARY falls back on MRS. MOUNTCHESSINGTON and GEORGINA]*

Curtain.

Scene 2

Library in Trenchard Manor. Oriel window, left center, with curtains. Two chairs and a table are brought on at change.
Enter BINNY and COYLE, left.

BINNY: Sir Hedward will see you directly, Mr. Coyle.

COYLE: Very well. House full of company, I see, Mr. Binny.

BINNY: Cram full, Mr. Coyle. As one of the first families in the country we must keep up our position.

COYLE *[Rubbing his hands]:*   Certainly, certainly, that is as long as we can, Mr. Binny. Tell Murcott, my clerk, to bring my papers in here. You'll find him in the servants' hall, and see that you keep your strong ale out of his way. People who serve me must have their senses about them.

BINNY *[Aside]:*   I should say so, or 'e'd 'ave hevery tooth hout in their 'eds, the wiper. *[Exit, left]*

COYLE: And now to show this pompous baronet the precipice on which he stands.

Enter MURCOTT, with green bag and papers.

COYLE: Are you sober, sirrah?

MURCOTT: Yes, Mr. Coyle.

COYLE: Then see you keep so.

MURCOTT: I'll do my best, sir. But, oh! Do tell them to keep liquor out of my way. I can't keep from it now, try as I will, and I try hard enough, God help me!

COYLE: Pshaw! Get out those mortgages and the letters from my London agent. *[MURCOTT takes papers from bag and places them on the table. COYLE looks off, right]* So. Here comes Sir Edward. Go, but be within call. I may want you to witness a signature.

MURCOTT: I will, sir. *[Aside]* I must have brandy, or my hand will not be steady enough to write. *[Exit, right]*

Enter SIR EDWARD, right. COYLE bows.

SIR EDWARD: Good morning, Coyle, good morning. *[With affected ease]* There is a chair, Coyle. *[They sit]* So you see those infernal trades people are pretty troublesome.

COYLE: My agent's letter this morning announces that Walter and Brass have got judgment and execution on their amount for repairing your town house last season. *[Refers to papers]* Boquet and Barker announce their intention of taking this same course with the wine account. Handmarth is preparing for a settlement of his heavy demand for the stables. Then there is Temper for pictures and other things, and Miss Florence Trenchard's account with Madame Pompon, and—

SIR EDWARD: Confound it, why harass me with details, these infernal particulars. Have you made out the total?

COYLE: Four thousand, eight hundred and thirty pounds, nine shillings and sixpence.

SIR EDWARD: Well, of course we must find means of settling this extortion.

COYLE: Yes, Sir Edward, if possible.

SIR EDWARD: If possible?

COYLE: I, as your agent, must stoop to detail, you must allow me to repeat, if possible.

SIR EDWARD: Why, you don't say there will be any difficulty in raising the money?

COYLE: What means would you suggest, Sir Edward?

SIR EDWARD: That, sir, is your business.

COYLE: A foretaste in the interest on the Fanhill and Ellenthrope mortgages, you are aware both are in arrears, the mortgagees, in fact, write here their intentions to foreclose. *[Shows papers]*

SIR EDWARD: Curse your impudence; pay them off.

COYLE: How, Sir Edward?

SIR EDWARD: Confound it, sir, which of us is the agent? Am I to find you brains for your own business?

COYLE: No, Sir Edward, I can furnish the brains, but what I ask of you is to furnish the money.

SIR EDWARD: There must be money somewhere. I came into possession of one of the finest properties in Hampshire only twenty-six years ago, and now you mean to tell me I cannot raise 4,000 pounds?

COYLE: The fact is distressing, Sir Edward, but so it is.

SIR EDWARD: There's the Ravensdale property unencumbered.

COYLE: There, Sir Edward, you are under a mistake. The Ravensdale property is deeply encumbered, to nearly its full value.

SIR EDWARD *[Springing up]:*   Good heavens.

COYLE: I have found among my father's papers a mortgage of that very property to him.

SIR EDWARD: To your father! My father's agent?

COYLE: Yes, bearing date the year after the great contested election for the county, on which the late Sir Edward patriotically spent sixty thousand pounds for the honor of not being returned to Parliament.

SIR EDWARD: A mortgage on the Ravensdale estate. But it must have been paid off, Mr. Coyle, *[Anxiously]* have you looked for the release or the receipt?

COYLE: Neither exists. My father's sudden death explains sufficiently I was left in ignorance of the transaction, but the seals on the deed and the stamps are intact; here is, sir. *[Shows it]*

SIR EDWARD: Sir, do you know that if this be true I am something like a beggar, and your father something like a thief.

COYLE: I see the first plainly, Sir Edward, but not the second.

SIR EDWARD: Do you forget, sir, that your father was a charity boy, fed, clothed by my father?

COYLE: Well, Sir Edward?

SIR EDWARD: And do you mean to tell me, sir, that your father repaid that kindness by robbing his benefactor?

COYLE: Certainly not, but by advancing money to that benefactor when he wanted it, and by taking the security of one of his benefactor's estates, as any prudent man would in the circumstances.

SIR EDWARD: Why, then, sir, the benefactor's property is yours.

COYLE: Pardon me, the legal estate; you have your equity of redemption. You have only to pay the money and the estate is yours as before.

SIR EDWARD: How dare you, sir, when you have just shown me that I cannot raise five hundred pounds in the world. Oh! Florence, why did I not listen to you when you warned me against this man?

COYLE *[Aside]*:   Oh! She warned you, did she? *[Aloud]* I see one means, at least, of keeping Ravensdale in the family.

SIR EDWARD: What is it?

COYLE: By marrying your daughter to the mortgagee.

SIR EDWARD: To you?

COYLE: I am prepared to settle the estate on Miss Trenchard the day she becomes Mrs. Richard Coyle.

SIR EDWARD *[Springing up]*:   You insolent scoundrel, how dare you insult me in my own house, sir! Leave it, sir, or I will have you kicked out by my servants.

COYLE: I never take an angry man at his word, Sir Edward. Give a few moments reflection to my offer; you can have me kicked out afterwards.

SIR EDWARD *[Pacing stage]*:   A beggar, Sir Edward Trenchard a beggar, see my children reduced to labor for their bread, to misery perhaps. But the alternative . . . Florence detests him, still the match would save *her,* at least, from ruin. He might take the family name, I might retrench, retire to the continent for a few years. Florence's health might serve as a pretense. Repugnant as the alternative is, yet it deserves consideration.

COYLE *[Who has watched]*:   Now, Sir Edward, shall I ring for the servants to kick me out?

SIR EDWARD: Nay, Mr. Coyle, you must pardon my outburst, you know I am hasty, and—

FLORENCE *[Without]*:   Papa, dear! *[Enters gaily, starts on seeing Coyle]* Papa, pardon my breaking in on business, but our American cousin has come—such an original—and we are only waiting for you to escort us to the field.

SIR EDWARD: I will come directly, my love. Mr. Coyle, my dear; you did not see him.

FLORENCE *[Disdainfully]*:   Oh, yes, I saw him, Papa.

SIR EDWARD: Nay, Florence, your hand to Mr. Coyle. *[Aside]* I insist.

FLORENCE: Papa. *[Frightened at his look, gives her hand. COYLE attempts to kiss it; she snatches it away and crosses to left]*

SIR EDWARD *[Crosses to left]:*   Come, Florence. Mr. Coyle, we will join you in the park. Come, my love, take my arm. *[Hurries her off, left]*

COYLE: Shallow, selfish fool. She warned you of me, did she? And you did not heed her; you both shall pay dearly. She, for her suspicions, and you that you did not share them. *[Walks up and down]* How lucky the seals were not cut from that mortgage when the release was given. 'Tis like the silly security of the Trenchards. This makes Ravensdale mine, while the release that restores it lies in the recess of the bureau, whose secret my father revealed to me on his death bed. *[Enter MURCOTT, left]* Write to the mortgagees of the Fanhill and Ellenthrope estates, to foreclose before the week is out, and tell Walters and Brass to put in execution today. We'll prick this wind-bag of a Baronet. Abel, we have both a bone to pick with him and his daughter. *[MURCOTT starts]* Why, what's the matter?

MURCOTT: Nothing, the dizziness I've had lately.

COYLE: Brandy in the evening, brandy in the morning, brandy all night. What a fool you are, Murcott.

MURCOTT: Who knows that as well as I do?

COYLE: If you would but keep the money out of your mouth, there's the making of a man in you yet.

MURCOTT: No, no, it's gone too far, thanks to the man who owns this house. You know all about it. How he found me a thriving, sober lad, flogging the village children through their spelling book. How he took a fancy to me as he called it and employed me here to teach his son and Miss Florence. *[His voice falters]* Then remember how I forgot who and what I was, and was cuffed out of the house like a dog. How I lost my school, my good name, but still hung about the place, they all looked askance at me—you don't know how that kills the heart of a man—then I took to drink and sank down, down, until I came to this.

COYLE: You owe Sir Edward revenge, do you not? You shall have a rare revenge on him. That mortgage you found last week puts the remainder of the property in my reach, and I close my hand on it unless he will consent to my terms.

MURCOTT: You can drive a hard bargain, I know.

COYLE: And a rare price I ask for his forebearance, Abel—his daughter's hand.

MURCOTT: Florence?

COYLE: Yes, Florence marries Richard Coyle. Richard Coyle steps into Sir Edward's estates. There, you dog, will not that be a rare revenge! So follow me with those papers. *[Crosses to left]* And now to lay the mine that will topple over the pride of the Trenchards. *[Exit, left]*

MURCOTT: He marry Florence! Florence Trenchard! My Florence. Mine! Florence *his* wife. No, no better a thousand time she had been mine, low as I am, when I dreampt that dream, but it shan't be, it shan't be. *[Tremblingly putting papers in bag]* If I can help her, sot though I am. Yes, I can help her, if the shock don't break me down. Oh! My poor muddled brain, surely there was a release with it when I found it. I must see Florence to warn her and expose Coyle's villainy. Oh! How my poor head throbs when I try to move. I shall die if I don't have a drop of brandy, yes, brandy. *[Exit, left]*

Scene 3

Inner chamber at Trenchard Manor. Large shower bath near right. Toilet table with drawer, left. Small bottle in drawer with red sealing wax on cork. ASA discovered seated, right. with foot on table, smoking a cigar. Valise on floor in front of him. BINNY discovered standing by his side.

ASA: Wal, I guess I begin to feel kinda comfortable here in this place, if it warn't for this 'tarnal fat critter. He don't seem to have any work to do, but swells out his big bosom like an old turkey-cock in laying time. I do wonder what he's here for. Do they think I mean to absquatulate with the spoons? *[BINNY attempts to take valise; ASA puts his foot on it]* Let that sweat. That's my plunder.

BINNY: Will you have the kindness to give me your keys, hif you please, sir?

Asa: What do you want with my keys?

Binny: To put your things away in the wardrobe, sir.

Asa: Wal, I calkalate if my two shirts, three bosoms, four collars, and two pairs of socks were to get into that everlasting big bunk, they'd think themselves so all-fired small I should never be able to crawl into them again.

Binny: Will you take a baath before you dress.

Asa: Take a baath?

Binny: A baath.

Asa: I suppose you mean a bath. Wal, man, I calkalate I ain't going to expose myself to the shakes by getting into cold water in this cruel cold climate of yours; so make tracks.

Binny: Make what?

Asa: Vamose!

Binny: Make vamose?

Asa: Absquatulate.

Binny: Ab—what sir?

Asa: Skedaddle.

Binny: Skedaddle?

Asa: Oh! Get out.

Binny: Oh! *[Going]* If you are going to dress you'll want some hassistance.

Asa: Assistance! What, to get out of my unmentionables and into them again? Wal, 'spose I do, what then?

Binny: Just ring the bell. Hi'll hattend you.

Asa: All right, come along. *[Binny going]* Hold on: say, I may want to yawn presently and shall want somebody to shut my mouth. *[Binny hurries off, left]* Wal, now I am alone, I can look about me and indulge the enquiring spirit of an American citizen. What an everlasting lot of things and fixin's there is to be sure. *[Opens table drawer]* Here's a place will hold my plunder beautifully. *[Sees bottle]* Hallo, what's this? *[Comes down]* Something good to drink. *[Smells bottle]* It smells awful bad. *[Reads label]* Golden Fluid; one application turns the hair a beautiful brown, several applications will turn the hair a lustrous black. Well, if they keep on it may turn a pea green. I reckon this has been left here by some fellow who is ashamed of his top knot. *[Knock]* Come in.

Enter BINNY, left.

BINNY: Mr. Buddicombe, sir, my lord's hown man.

ASA: Roll him in. *[BINNY beckons. Enter BUDDICOMBE]* Turkey cock number two, what is it?

BUDDICOMBE: My Lord Dundreary's compliments, and *have* you seen a small *bottle* in the toilet table drawer?

ASA: Suppose I had, what then?

BUDDICOMBE: My lord wants it partic'ly.

ASA: Was it a small bottle?

BINNY: Bottle small.

ASA: Blue label?

BINNY: Label blue.

ASA: Red sealing wax on the top?

BUDDICOMBE: Red sealing wax.

BINNY: Wax red.

ASA: Nice little bottle?

BINNY: Little bottle nice.

ASA: Wal, I ain't seen it. *[Aside]* If my lord sets a valley on it, guess it must be worth something.

BUDDICOMBE: Sorry to trouble you, sir.

BINNY *[Aside to BUDDICOMBE]:* What his hit?

BUDDICOMBE: My lord's hair dye, the last bottle, and he turns red tomorrow. *[Exit in haste]*

BINNY: 'Orrible, what a hawful situation, to be sure.

ASA *[Aside]:* So I've got my ring in that lord's nose, and if I don't make him dance to my tune it's a pity.

BINNY: Miss Florence begged me to say she had borrowed a costume for you, for the harchery meeting, sir.

ASA: Hain't you dropped something?

BINNY: Where?

ASA: What do you mean by the harchery meeting?

BINNY: Where they shoot with bows and harrows.

ASA: There goes another of them! You needn't look for them; you can't find them when you want 'em. Now you just take my compliments to Miss Trenchard; when I goes out shooting with injurious weapons I always wears my own genuine shooting costume. That's the natural buff tipped off with a little red paint.

BINNY: Good gracious, he'd look like Hadam and Heve, in the garden of Eden. *[Exit]*

ASA: Wal, there's a queer lot of fixin's. *[Sees shower bath]* What on airth is that? Looks like a 'skeeter net, only it ain't long enough for a fellow to lay down in unless he was to coil himself up like a woodchuck in a knot hole. I'd just like to know what the all-fired thing is meant for. *[Calls]* Say, Puffy, Puffy. Oh! He told me if I wanted him to ring the bell. *[Looks around room]* Where on airth is the bell? *[Slips partly in shower bath, pulls rope, water comes down]* Murder! Help! Fire! Water! I'm drownin'!

Enter SKILLET, SHARPE, right. BINNY, BUDDICOMBE, left. Seeing ASA, all laugh, and keep it up till curtain falls.

ACT TWO

Scene 1

Oriel Chamber.

Enter Mrs. Mountchessington *and* Augusta, *left, dressed for archery meeting.*

Mrs. Mount: Well, Augusta, what think you of our American cousin?

Augusta: He is a very uncouth, ridiculous fellow.

Mrs. Mount: But my dear, you must remember that he has inherited all of old Mark Trenchard's property. And though he may appear rude in his manner, I want you to appear well in his eyes. I don't by any means want you to give up De Boots; his expectations are excellent, and should you fail with Mr. Trenchard you will have him to fall back upon. But, pray be attentive to this American savage, as I rather think he will prove the better match of the two.

Augusta *[Disdainfully]*:   Yes, Ma.

Mrs. Mount: And look more cheerful, my love.

Augusta: I am so tired, Ma, of admiring things I hate.

Mrs. Mount: Yes, my poor love, yet we must all make sacrifices to society. Look at your poor sister, with the appetite.

Augusta: What am I to be enthusiastic about with that American, Ma?

Mrs. Mount: Oh! I hardly know yet, my dear. We must study him. I think if you read up on Sam Slick a little, it might be useful, and just dip into Bancroft's History of the United States, or some of Russell's Letters; you should know something of George Washington, of whom the Americans are justly proud.

Augusta: Here he comes, Ma. What a ridiculous figure he looks in that dress, ha! Ha!

Mrs. Mount: Hush, my dear.

Enter Asa, *in archery dress.*

AUGUSTA: Oh, Mr. Trenchard, why did you not bring me one of those lovely Indian's dresses of your boundless prairie?

MRS. MOUNT: Yes, one of those dresses in which you hunt the buffalo.

AUGUSTA *[Extravagantly]:*   Yes, in which you hunt the buffalo.

ASA *[Imitating]:*   In which I hunt the buffalo. *[Aside]* Buffalo down in Vermont! *[Aloud]* Wal, you see, them dresses are principally the nateral skin, tipped off with paint, and the Indians object to parting with them.

BOTH: Ahem! Ahem!

ASA: The first buffalo I see about here I shall hunt up for you.

MRS. MOUNT: Oh, you Americans are so clever, and so acute.

AUGUSTA: Yes, so 'cute.

ASA: Yes, we're cute, we are; know soft solder when we see it.

AUGUSTA *[Aside]:*   Ma, I do believe he's laughing at us.

MRS. MOUNT: Oh, no, my dear, you are mistaken. Oh! I perceive they are appearing for the archery practice. I suppose we shall see you on the ground, Mr. Trenchard.

ASA: Which?

MRS. MOUNT: Au revoir. *[Exits with* AUGUSTA, *right]*

ASA: No, thank you, don't take any before dinner. No use their talking Dutch to me. Wal, I never seed an old gal stand fire like that. She's a real old bison bull. I feel all-fired tuckered out riding in those keers. I'd like to have a snooze if I could find a place to lay down in. *[Sees curtain on window, left]* Oh, this might do! *[Pulls curtain, then starts back]* No you don't! One shower bath a day is enough for me. *[Cautiously opens them]* No, I guess this is all right, I shall be as snug in here as a pew at meeting, or a private box at the theatre. Hello! Somebody's coming. *[Goes into recess]*

Enter DUNDREARY *and* BUDDICOMBE, *left.*

BUDDICOMBE: My lord—

DUNDREARY: *[Business]*

BUDDICOMBE: My lord!

DUNDREARY: *[Business]*

BUDDICOMBE: Your lordship *[Louder]*

DUNDREARY: There, now you've spoiled it.

BUDDICOMBE: Spoiled what, my lord?

DUNDREARY: Spoiled what, my lord; why, a most magnificent sneeze!

BUDDICOMBE: I am very sorry, my lord.

DUNDREARY: Now that I can speak alone with you, tell me about that hair dye. Have you found it?

BUDDICOMBE: Not a trace of it, my lord.

DUNDREARY: If you don't find it, I'll discharge you.

BUDDICOMBE: Very well, my lord. *[Bows and exits, left]*

DUNDREARY: Very well, my lord! He's gone and lost my hair dye, and my hair turns red tomorrow, and when I ask him to find it for me or I'll discharge him, he says, "Very well, my lord." He's positively idiotic, he is—Ah! Here comes Miss Georgina, that gorgeous creature—that lovely sufferer. *[Exit, left]*

ASA *[Looking out]:*   What's the price of hair dye? Hallo! He's coming again with that sick girl.

Re-enter DUNDREARY and GEORGINA, left.

DUNDREARY: Will you try and strengthen your limbs with a gentle walk in the garden?

GEORGINA: No thank you, my lord. I'm so delicate. Oh, my lord, it is so painful to walk languidly through life, to be unable, at times, to bear the perfumes of one's favorite flowers. Even those violets you sent me yesterday I was compelled to have removed from my room, the perfume was too strong for me. I'm so delicate.

DUNDREARY: Yes, they're pretty flowers; if only they were a different color. But they're very strengthening flowers, you know.

GEORGINA: Yes, my lord, you are always right.

DUNDREARY: Do you know I'm getting to be very robust?

GEORGINA: Would I could share that fault with you; but I am so delicate.

DUNDREARY: If you were robust I should not love you as I do. It would deprive you of that charm which enchains me to your lovely side, which—which—

GEORGINA: Oh, my lord, my lord! I'm going to faint.

DUNDREARY: And I'm going to sneeze; you faint while I sneeze.

GEORGINA *[Taking his arm]:*   Oh! my lord.

DUNDREARY: Do you know what a sneeze is?

GEORGINA: No, my lord.

DUNDREARY: Did you ever sneeze?

GEORGINA: No, my lord.

DUNDREARY: She never sneezed. I'll tell what a sneeze is: Imagine a very large spider.

GEORGINA *[Screams]*: Where, my lord?

DUNDREARY: No, no, I don't mean a real spider, only an imaginary one, a large spider getting up your nose, and all of a sudden, much to his disgust, he discovers he has put his foot in it and can't get it out again.

GEORGINA: That must be very distressing.

DUNDREARY: For the spider, yes, and not very pleasant for the nose.

GEORGINA: Oh! My lord, do take me to Mamma.

DUNDREARY: No, you lovely sufferer, let's walk a little more.

GEORGINA: I can't, my lord, I'm *so* delicate.

DUNDREARY: Well, then, exercise, imitate that little hop of mine. *[Hops]* It isn't a run, it's a—

GEORGINA: What is it?

DUNDREARY: No, it isn't a what-is-it. Well, let me suppose I get you an oyster. *[GEORGINA shakes her head]* Oh! Then suppose I get you an oyster.

GEORGINA: No, my lord, I'm too delicate.

DUNDREARY: How would you like the left wing of a canary bird?

GEORGINA: No, my lord, it's too strong for me.

DUNDREARY: Let me ask you a widdle—why does a duck go under water? For divers reasons. Now I'll give you another.—why does a duck come out of the water? For sundry reasons. No! No! See, you live on suction, you're like that bird with a long bill, they call doctor—no, that's not it; I thought it was a doctor because it has a long bill—I mean a snipe—yes, you're a lovely snipe. *[Exeunt, right]*

ASA: There goes a load of wooden nutmegs. Hello, here comes somebody else.

Enter FLORENCE, right, with paper.

FLORENCE *[Reads]*: 'One who still remembers what he ought long since to have forgotten, wishes to speak with Miss Trenchard'—'Florence' scratched out—'on matters of life and death, near the Oriel, in the west gallery'. Written upon a dirty sheet of paper, in a hardly legible hand. What does this mean; it opens like one of Miss Radcliffe's romances. Well, here I am, and now for my correspondent.

Enter MURCOTT, left.

MURCOTT: Oh, for one minute's clear head, Miss Florence.

FLORENCE: I presume you are the writer of this?

MURCOTT: Yes, I am.

FLORENCE: You address me as an old acquaintance, but I do not recognize you.

MURCOTT: So much the better. So much the better.

FLORENCE: I hate mystery, sir; but you see I have come to rendezvous. I must know to whom I am speaking.

MURCOTT: As frank as ever. I am Abel Murcott.

FLORENCE *[Starting back]:*   You?

MURCOTT: Do not be ashamed; I have not the strength to injure you, if I had the evil. In this shabby, broken down drunkard, you need not fear the madman, who years ago forgot in his frantic passion the gulf that lay between your station and his own. I am harmless except to myself.

FLORENCE: I fear no danger. Speak on, sir; I hear you.

MURCOTT: I need not tell you by what steps I came to this. You don't know, maybe you never knew, what a maddening thing a passion is when it turns against itself. After being expelled from my tutorship in this house, I lost my employment, self-respect, hope. I sought to drown recollection and draw courage from drink. It only embittered remembrances, and destroyed the little courage I had left. That I have bread to eat, I owe to Mr. Coyle; he employed me as his clerk. You know he has been with your father this morning. I have come to tell you my errand; are you as brave as you used to be when I knew—

FLORENCE: I fear nothing.

MURCOTT: I come to tell you of your father's ruin, his utter ruin.

FLORENCE: My father's ruin? What? What?

MURCOTT: His estates are mortgaged, his creditors clamorous. The bailiffs will be in Trenchard Manor today, disguised as your own servants. This much Mr. Coyle has conceded to your father's respect for appearances.

FLORENCE: Then beggary stares him in the face. Poor Father, what a sad blow for him. Is that all, sir?

MURCOTT: No; the worst remains.

FLORENCE: Go on, sir.

MURCOTT: Coyle knows your father's weakness and as a means of escape from ruin, to the verge of which he has brought him, he has this day proposed for your hand.

FLORENCE: Mine!

MURCOTT: On consideration of settling on you the Ravensdale Estate.

FLORENCE: And my father, how did he listen to such insolence?

MURCOTT: You know as well as I do how he would hear such a proposal: at first a torrent of rage, then the strong ebb of selfishness set in, and he consented to listen to the terms, to view them as something to be considered, to consider them.

FLORENCE: Good heavens, can this be true? No, I will not believe it of my father, and from such lips.

MURCOTT: You have full right to think this and to say it, but mark your father and Coyle today. You will then see if I speak the truth or not.

FLORENCE: Forgive my distrust, Mr. Murcott.

MURCOTT: I am past taking offense or feeling scorn; I have carried more than can be heaped upon me, but I did not come only to give you warning of your danger.

FLORENCE: Can you avert it?

ASA [*Coming down between them*]: Wal, stranger, that's just the question I was going to ask.

FLORENCE: You here, sir, and listening.

ASA: Wal, it wasn't on purpose. I went in there to take a snooze, I heard you talking and I thought it wouldn't be polite of me not to listen to what you had to say. I'm a rough sort of customer, and don't know much about the ways of great folks. But I've got a cool head, a stout arm, and a willing heart, and am grit to the back bone, and I think I can help you, just as one cousin ought to help another.

FLORENCE: Well, I do think you are honest.

MURCOTT: Shall I go on?

FLORENCE: Yes, we will trust him. Go on.

MURCOTT: I found the Ravensdale mortgage while rummaging in an old deed box of Coyle's father's; there was a folded paper inside the deed. I took both to Coyle unopened, like a besotted fool that I was. My belief is strong that the paper was the release of the mortgage, declaring that the money had been paid off, and the release executed without the seals having been cut from the original mortgage. I have known such things to happen.

ASA: Have ye, now? Well, if a Yankee had done such a thing he would have Judge Lynch after him in no time.

MURCOTT: If you can but find that release, we may unmask this diabolical fiend and save you.

FLORENCE: But, surely, a villain of Coyle's stability would have destroyed the paper, the very key-stone of his fraud.

MURCOTT: I fear so.

ASA: Do, you, now. Wal, you're wrong; you're both wrong. I guess you ain't either of you done much ciphering of human nature. The key-stone of their fraud is the the point your mighty cute rascals always leave unsecured. Come along with me, stranger, and we'll just work up this sum a little; two heads are better than one. Yours is a little muddled, but mine's pretty clear, and if I don't circumvent that old sarpint, Coyle—

FLORENCE: Well?

ASA: Say I am a skunk, that's all, and that's the meanest kind of an animal.

FLORENCE: I owe you much, Mr. Murcott, more than I can ever repay.

MURCOTT: No, no, no, if you did but know, the hope of seeing you has roused all the manhood that drink and misery has left me. God bless you, Miss Florence.

FLORENCE: No, you don't; call me Florence as you did when I was the truant pupil and you the indulgent tutor. *[Offers her hand]*

MURCOTT: No, no; for heaven's sake do not call back that time or I shall go mad! mad! mad! *[Rushes off, left, followed by FLORENCE]*

Scene 2

Park. Rural cottage, left, adjoining which, and projecting on stage, an inside view of a dairy with a sloping roof; backing painted to look like milk pans. The whole scene should have a picturesque appearance. Garden fence runs across back, ornamental gate or archway, right. Pigeon house on pole near dairy, left center. Spinning wheel inside cottage door, one or two rustic benches, right and left.

Enter WICKENS, right, with two milk pails on a yoke. Puts them down near dairy, then looks off, right.

WICKENS: There they go! That's a bull's eye, I warrant. Dang me, though, if I wouldn't rather see Miss Mary than that cock robin sport yonder. Here she comes. Good morning, Miss Mary. *[Enter MARY from cottage, left]*

MARY: Oh, Wickens, you are there. How kind of you to help me with the milk pails to-day, when all the lads and lasses have given themselves a holiday to see the shooting.

WICKENS: Ah, Miss Mary, you ought to be among them, with a green hat and feather, if all had their rights.

MARY *[Laughing]:*   Nay, ladies without a farthing in the world ought to put aside their ladyships; besides I'm proud of my dairy here. Just help me with this troublesome fellow; steady, don't shake it. The cream is foaming so beautifully. There. *[WICKENS carries pail into cottage and returns, down right]*

WICKENS: Now, Miss Mary, what can I do for you?

MARY: Let me see; well, really, I do believe, Wickens, I've nothing to do but amuse myself.

WICKENS: Dang it, Miss, that's a pity, 'cos I can't help you at that, you see.

MARY: Oh, yes! Bring me out dear old Welch nurse's spinning wheel *[Exit WICKENS into cottage, left]* There, that will do famously. I can catch the full scent of the jessamines.

WICKENS: *[Right center]:*   Anything more, Miss Mary?

MARY: No, thank you, Wickens.

WICKENS *[Returning]:*   Is there anything I can get for you, Miss Mary?

MARY *[Spinning]:*   Nothing, thank you.

WICKENS: Dang me if I wouldn't like to stop all day, and watch her pretty figure and run errands for her. *[Exit, right. Crosses behind fence]*

MARY: Poor Wickens is not the only one who thinks I am a very ill-used young body. Now I don't think so. Grandfather was rich, but he must have had a hard heart, or he never could have cast off poor Mamma. Had he adopted me, I should never have been so happy as I am now. Uncle is kind to me in his pompous, patronizing way, and dear Florence loves me like a sister; and so I am happy. I am my own mistress here, and not anybody's humble servant. I sometimes find myself singing as the birds do, because I can't help it.

Song, "Maid with the Milking Pail," can be introduced here. Enter FLORENCE *and* ASA *through gate, right.*

FLORENCE: Come along, cousin, come along. I want to introduce you to my little cousin. *[Kisses* MARY*]* I've brought you a visitor, Miss Mary Meredith. Mr. Asa Trenchard, our American cousin. *[They shake hands]* That will do for the present. This young gentleman has carried off the prize by three successive shots in the bull's eye.

MARY: I congratulate you, sir, and am happy to see you.

ASA *[Shakes hands again]:* Thank you, Miss.

FLORENCE: That . . . will do for a beginning.

ASA *[Aside]:* And so that is Mark Trenchard's grandchild.

MARY: Why have you left the archery, Florence?

FLORENCE: Because, after Mr. Asa's display, I felt in no humor for shooting, and I have some very grave business with my cousin here.

MARY: You? Grave business? Why I thought you never had any graver business than being very pretty, very amiable, and very ready to be amused.

ASA: Wal, Miss, I guess the first comes natural round these diggin's. *[Bows]*

MARY: You are very polite. This is my domain, sir, and I shall be happy to show you, that is, if you understand anything about a dairy.

FLORENCE: Yes. By the way, do you understand anything about dairies in America?

ASA: Wal, I guess I do know something about cow juice. *[They turn to smother laugh]* Why, if it ain't as bright and clean as a fresh washed shirt just off the clover, and is this all your doin's, Miss?

MARY: Yes, sir. I milk these cows, set up the milk, superintend the churning and make the cheese.

ASA: Wal, darn me if you ain't the first raal right down useful gal I've seen on this side of the pond.

FLORENCE: What's that, sir? Do you want to make me jealous?

ASA: Oh, no, you needn't get your back up. You are just the right sort too, but you must own you're small potatoes, and few in a hill compared to a gal like that.

FLORENCE: I'm what?

ASA: Small potatoes.

FLORENCE: Will you be kind enough to translate that for me, for I don't understand American yet.

ASA: Yes, I'll put it in French for you: "petites pommes de terres."

FLORENCE: Ah, it's very clear now. But, cousin, do tell me what you mean by calling me "small potatoes."

ASA: Wal, you can sing and paint, and play on the pianner, and in your own particular circle you are some pumpkins.

FLORENCE: Some pumpkins. First I am small potatoes, and now I'm some pumpkins.

ASA: But she, she can milk cows, set up the butter, make cheese, and, darn me, if them ain't what I call real downright feminine accomplishments.

FLORENCE: I do believe you are right, cousin; so, Mary, do allow me to congratulate you upon not being small potatoes.

MARY: Well, I must look to my dairy or all my last week's milk will be spoiled. Good-bye, Florence, dear. Good-bye, Mr. Trenchard. Good morning, sir. *[Exit into cottage]*

ASA *[Following her to door]:* Good morning, Miss. I'll call again.

FLORENCE: Well, cousin, what do you think of her?

ASA: Ain't she a regular snorter?

FLORENCE: A what?

ASA: I tell you that girl is a plum bird on a lily root. And to think I'm keepin' that everlasting angel of a girl out of her fortune all along of this bit of paper here.

FLORENCE: What is that?

ASA: Old Mark Trenchard's will.

FLORENCE: Don't show it to me; I don't want to look at it. The fortune should have come to Mary; she is the only relation in the direct line.

ASA: Say, cousin, you've not told her that darned property was left to me, have you?

FLORENCE: No, I hadn't the heart to do it.

ASA: Wal, darn me if you didn't show your good sense that time anyhow. *[Goes up to dairy]*

FLORENCE: Well, what are you doing, showing *your* good sense?

ASA: Oh, you go 'long.

FLORENCE: Say, cousin, I guess I've got a string on you now, as I heard you say this morning.

ASA: Now you git out! Didn't I see you casting sheep's eyes at that sailor man this morning? Ah, I reckon I've got *you* on a string now. Say, has he got that ship yet?

FLORENCE: No, he hasn't, though I've used all my powers of persuasion with that Lord Dundreary, and his father has so much influence with the Admiralty.

ASA: Wal, don't he drop like a smoked 'possum.

FLORENCE: There you go, more American. No, he said he was very sorry, but he couldn't.

ASA *[Taking bottle out]:* Oh, he did, did he? Wal, I guess he'll do his best all the same.

FLORENCE: I shall be missed at the archery grounds. Will you take me back?

ASA: Like a streak of lightning. *[Offers arm and takes her to dairy]*

FLORENCE: Well, but where are you going now?

ASA: I was just going 'round. I say, cousin, do you think you could find your way back alone?

FLORENCE: Why, what do *you* want to do?

ASA: Wal, I just wanted to see how they make cheese in this darned country. *[Exits into dairy]*

FLORENCE *[Laughing]:* And they call that man a savage! Well, I only wish we had a few more such savages in England.

DUNDREARY *[Without, right]:* This way, lovely sufferer.

FLORENCE: Ah, here's Dundreary.

DUNDREARY enters with GEORGINA, places her in a rustic chair, right.

DUNDREARY: There, repothe yourself.

GEORGINA: Thank you, my lord. You are so kind to me, and I am so delicate.

FLORENCE: Yes, you look delicate, dear. How is she this morning? Any better?

DUNDREARY: When she recovers, she'll be better.

FLORENCE: I'm afraid you don't take good care of her, you are so rough.

DUNDREARY: No, I'm not wruff, either *[Sings]* I'm gentle and I'm kind, I'm—I forget the rest.

FLORENCE: Well, good morning, dear—do take care of her—good day, Dundreary. *[Exit through gate]*

DUNDREARY: Now, let me administer to your wants. How would you like a roast chestnut?

GEORGINA: No, my lord. I'm too delicate.

DUNDREARY: Well, then, a peanut; there is a great deal of nourishment in peanuts.

GEORGINA: No, thank you.

DUNDREARY: Then what can I do for you?

GEORGINA: If you please, ask the dairy maid to let me have a seat in the dairy. I am afraid of the draft here.

{DUNDREARY: Don't be alarmed; there is no more draft.}[3]   Is that the dairy on top of that stick? *[Points to pigeon house]*

GEORGINA: No, my lord; that's the pigeon house.

DUNDREARY: What do they keep in pigeon houses? Oh! Pigeons, to be sure; they couldn't keep donkeys up there, could they? That's the dairy, I suppothe?

GEORGINA: Yes, my lord.

DUNDREARY: What do they keep in dairies?

GEORGINA: Eggs, milk, butter and cheese.

DUNDREARY: What's the name of that animal with a head on it? No, I don't mean that; all animals have heads. I mean those animals with something growing out of their heads.

GEORGINA: A cow?

---

3. This line was ad-libbed by Dundreary (E. A. Emerson) during the April 14, 1865 performance at Ford's.

DUNDREARY: A cow growing out of his head?

GEORGINA: No, no, horns.

DUNDREARY: A cow! Well, that accounts for the milk and butter; but I don't see the eggs; cows don't give eggs. Then there's the cheese—do you like cheese?

GEORGINA: No, my lord.

DUNDREARY: Does your brother like cheese?

GEORGINA: I have no brother. I'm so delicate.

DUNDREARY: Did I ever tell you about Sam, my brother Sam?

GEORGINA: About Sam? No, my Lord.

DUNDREARY: You would have liked Sam—he never had a 'uel—he was rather an ass, but you would have liked him.

GEORGINA: I have no doubt I should, for they say he is very much like you.

DUNDREARY: Yes. Oh, he's a pretty nice fellow. He went off to America. Sam wanted to see the world; he thought it would enlarge his mind, and all that sort of nonsense. But he'd better have stopped at home. Yes, he got shipwrecked in the Pacific Ocean and had nothing to eat for 57 days.

GEORGINA *[Puts hand to stomach]:*   Do please take me to the dairy.

DUNDREARY: Well, I will see if I can get you a broiled sardine. *[Exit into dairy]*

GEORGINA *[Jumps up]:*   Oh! I'm so glad he's gone. I'm so dreadful hungry. I should like a plate of corn beef and cabbage, eggs and bacon, or a slice of cold ham and pickles.

DUNDREARY *[Outside]:*   Thank you, thank you.

GEORGINA *[Running back to seat]:*   Here he comes. Oh! I'm so delicate.

Enter DUNDREARY.

DUNDREARY: I beg your pardon, Miss Georgina, but I find upon enquiry that cows don't give sardines. But I've arranged it with the dairy maid that you can have a seat by the window that overlooks the cow house and the pig sty, and all the pretty things.

GEORGINA: I'm afraid I'm very troublesome.

DUNDREARY: Yes, you're very troublesome, you are. No, I mean you're a lovely sufferer, that's the idea. *[They go up to cottage door]*

Enter Asa, running against Dundreary.

Dundreary: There's that damned rhinocerous again. *[Exit into cottage with Georgina]*

Asa: There goes that benighted aristocrat and that little toad of a sick gal. *[Looks off]* There, he's a settling her into a chair and covering her all over with shawls. Ah! It's a caution, how these women do fix our flint for us. Here he comes. *[Takes out bottle]* How are you, hair dye? *[Goes behind dairy]*

Enter Dundreary.

Dundreary: That lovely Georgina puts me in mind of that beautiful piece of poetry. Let me see how it goes: The rose is red, the violet's blue. *[Asa tips his hat over his eyes]*

Dundreary *[Repeats]*   Asa *[Repeats business]*

Dundreary *[Comes down, takes Asa's hat off, looks in it]:*   There must be something alive in that hat. *[Goes up and commences again]* The rose is red, the violet's blue, sugar is sweet, and so is somebody, and so is somebody else.

Asa puts yoke on Dundreary's shoulders gently. Dundreary comes down with pails.

Dundreary: I wonder what the devil that is? *[Lowers one, then the other; they trip him up]* Oh, I see somebody has been fishing and caught a pail. *[Goes hopping up stage, stumbling over against spinning wheel. Looks at yarn on stick]* Why, what a little old man. *[Sees Asa]* Say, Mr. Exile, what the devil is this?

Asa: That is a steam engine, and will bust in about a minute.

Dundreary: Well, I haven't a minute to spare, so I'll not wait till it busts. *[Crosses to right, knocks against private box, right, apologizes]*

Asa: Say, whiskers, I want to ask a favor of you.

Dundreary *[Attempts to sneeze]:*   Now I've got it.

Asa: Wal, but say. *[Dundreary's sneezing business]*

Asa *[Takes his hand]:*   How are you? *[Squeezes his hand]*

Dundreary: There, you've spoiled it.

Asa: Spoiled what?

Dundreary: Spoiled what! Why, a magnificent sneeze.

Asa: Oh! Was that what you were trying to get through you?

Dundreary: Get through me! He's mad.

ASA: Wal, now, the naked truth is—*[Leans arm on DUNDREARY'S shoulder. Business by DUNDREARY]* Oh, come, now. Don't be putting on airs. Say, do you know Lieut. Vernon?

DUNDREARY: Slightly.

ASA: Wal, what do you think of him on an average?

DUNDREARY: Think of a man on an average?

ASA: Wal, I think he's a real hoss, and he wants a ship.

DUNDREARY: Well, if he's a real hoss, he must want a carriage.

ASA: Darn me, if that ain't good.

DUNDREARY: That's good.

ASA: Yes, that is good.

DUNDREARY: Very good.

ASA: Very good, indeed, *for you.*

DUNDREARY: Now I've got it. *[Tries to sneeze]*

ASA: Wal, now I say. *[DUNDREARY trying to sneeze]*

DUNDREARY: What, are you at that again?

DUNDREARY business. ASA bites his finger. DUNDREARY goes up, stumbles against chair and comes down again.

DUNDREARY: I've got the influenza.

ASA: Got the what?

DUNDREARY: He says I've got a wart. I've got the influenza.

ASA: That's it exactly. I want your influence, sir, to get that ship.

DUNDREARY: That's good.

ASA: Yes, that's good, ain't it?

DUNDREARY: Very good.

ASA: Yes, darn me if that ain't good.

DUNDREARY: For you. Ha! Ha! One on that Yankee.

ASA: Well done, Britisher. Wal, now, how about that ship?

DUNDREARY: I want all my influence, sir, for my own w—w—welations. *[Stammering]*

ASA: Oh! You want it all for your own w—w—welations. *[Mincing]*

DUNDREARY: I say, sir. *[ASA pretends deafness. This business is ad lib]*

ASA: Eh?

DUNDREARY: He's hard of hearing, and thinks he's in a balloon. Mister.

Asa: Eh?

Dundreary: He thinks he can hear with his nose. I say—

Asa: Eh?

Dundreary turns Asa's nose around with his thumb. Asa puts his two hands up to Dundreary's.

Dundreary: Now he thinks he's a musical instrument. I say—

Asa: What?

Dundreary: You stutter. I'll give you a k—k—k—

Asa: No you won't give me a kick.

Dundreary: I'll give you a c—c—card to a doctor and he'll c—c-

Asa: No, he won't kick me either.

Dundreary: He's idiotic. I don't mean that; he'll cure you.

Asa: Same one that cured you?

Dundreary: The same.

Asa: Wal, if you're cured I want to stay sick. He must be a mighty smart man.

Dundreary: A very clever man, he is.

Asa: Wal, darn me, if there ain't a physiological change taking place. Your whiskers at this moment—

Dundreary: My whiskers!

Asa: Yes, about the ends they're black as niggers in biling time, and near the roots they're all speckled and streaked.

Dundreary *[Horror struck]*: My whiskers speckled and streaked?

Asa *[Showing bottle]*: Now, this is a wonderful invention.

Dundreary: My hair dye. My dear sir.

Asa *[Squeezing his hand]*: How are you?

Dundreary: Dear Mr. Trenchard.

Puts arm on shoulder. Asa repeats Dundreary business: putting on eye glass hopping around stage and stroking whiskers.

Dundreary: He's mad, he's deaf, he squints, stammers and he's a hopper.

Asa: Now, look here; you get the lieutenant a ship and I'll give you the bottle. It's a fine swap.

Dundreary: What the devil is a swap?

Asa: Well, you give me the ship, and I'll give you the bottle to boot.

Dundreary: What do I want of your boots? I haven't got a ship about me.

Asa: You'd better make haste or your whiskers will be changed again. They'll be pea green in about a minute.

Dundreary *[Crosses to left]*: Pea green! *[Exits hastily into house]*

Asa: I guess I've got a ring in his nose now. I wonder how that sick gal is getting along. Wal, darn me, if the dying swallow ain't pitching into ham and eggs and home-made bread. Wal, she's walking into the fodder like a farmer arter a day's work rail splitting. I'll just give her a start. How-de-do, Miss. Allow me to congratulate you on the return of your appetite. *[Georgina screams]* Guess I've got a ring in her pretty nose now. *[Looks off, right]* Hello! Here comes the lickers and shooters. It's about time I took my medicine, I reckon.

Enter, from right, Sir Edward, Mrs. Mountchessington, Florence, Vernon, Augusta, de Boots, Wickens, Coyle, Sharp, Binny, Skillet, Buddicombe, two servants in livery, carrying tray and glasses, a wine basket containing four bottles to represent champagne, knife to cut strings, some powerful acid in one bottle for Asa—pop sure.

Sir Edward: Now to distribute the prizes and drink to the health of the winner of the golden arrow.

Florence: And there stands the hero of the day. Come, kneel down.

Asa: Must I kneel down?

Florence: I am going to crown you Captain of the Archers of Trenchard Manor.

Asa *[Aside to Florence]*: I've got the ship.

Florence: No! Have you?

Sir Edward: Come, ladies and gentlemen; take from me. *[Takes glasses, starts on seeing men in livery]* Who are these strange faces?

Coyle *[In his ear]*: Bailiffs, Sir Edward.

Sir Edward: Bailiffs! Florence, I am lost.

Florence supports her father. At the same moment Dundreary enters with letter and money. Georgina appears at the door as Dundreary comes down, left. Asa cuts string of bottle; cork hits Dundreary. General commotion as curtain descends.

ACT THREE

Scene 1

Dairy set, as in preceding scene. ASA, discovered on bench, right center, whittling a stick. MARY, busy with milk pans in dairy.

ASA: Miss Mary, I wish you'd leave off those everlasting dairy fixin's, and come and take a hand of chat along with me.

MARY: What, and leave my work? Why, when you first came here, you thought I could not be too industrious.

ASA: Well, I think so yet, Miss Mary, but I've got a heap to say to you, and I never talk while you're moving about so spry among them pans, pails, and cheeses.

MARY *[Brings sewing down]:* Well, then, I'll sit here. *[Sits on bench with ASA, vis-á-vis]* Well now, will that do?

ASA: Well, no, Miss Mary, that won't do neither; them eyes of yourn takes my breath away.

MARY: What will I do, then?

ASA: Well, I don't know, Miss Mary, but, darn me, if you could do anything that wasn't so 'tarnal neat and handsome, that a fellow would want you to keep on doing nothing else all the time.

MARY: Well, then, I'll go away. *[Rises]*

ASA *[Stopping her]:* No, don't do that, Miss Mary; for then I'll be left in total darkness. *[She sits]* Somehow I feel kinder lost, if I haven't got you to talk to. Now that I've got the latitude and longitude of all them big folks, found out the length of every lady's foot, and the soft spot on everybody's head, they can't teach me nothing. But here, *[Whittling]* here I come to school.

MARY: Then throw away that stick, and put away your knife, like a good boy. *[Throws away stick up stage]* I must cure you of that dreadful trick of whittling.

ASA: Oh, if you only knew how it helps me to keep my eyes off you, Miss Mary.

MARY: But you needn't keep your eyes off me.

ASA: I'm afraid I must; my eyes are awful tale-tellers, and they might be saying something you wouldn't like to hear, and that might make you mad, and then you'd shut up school, and send me home feeling about as small as a tadpole with his tail bobbed off.

MARY: Don't be alarmed; I don't think I will listen to any tales that your eyes may tell unless they're tales I like and ought to hear.

ASA: If I thought they'd tell any other, Miss Mary, I'd pluck them out and throw them in the first turnip patch I came to.

MARY: And now tell me more about your home in America. Do you know I've listened to your stories until I'm half a backwoods-man's wife already?

ASA *[Aside]*: Wouldn't I like to make her a whole one!

MARY: Yes, I can shut my eyes and almost fancy your home in the backwoods. There are your two sisters running about in their sunbonnets.

ASA: Debby and Nab? Yes!

MARY: Then I can see the smoke curling from the chimney, then men and boys working in the fields.

ASA: Yes.

MARY: The girls milking the cows, and everybody so busy.

ASA: Yes.

MARY: And then at night, home to your four big brothers, laden with game, tired and foot sore, and covered with snow.

ASA: That's so.

MARY: Then how we lasses bustle about to prepare supper. The fire blazes on the hearth, while your good old mother cooks the slapjacks.

ASA *[Getting very excited]*: Yes!

MARY: And then after supper the lads and lasses go to a corn husking. The demijohn of old peach brandy is brought out and everything is so nice.

ASA: I shall faint in about five minutes. Miss Mary, you're a darned sight too good for this country. You ought to make tracks.

MARY: Make what?

ASA: Make tracks, pack up, and emigrate to the roaring old state of Vermont, and live 'long with mother. She'd make you so comfortable, and there would be sister Debby and Nab and, well, I reckon I'd be there, too.

MARY: Oh! I'm afraid if I were there your mother would find the poor English girl a sad encumbrance.

ASA: Oh, she ain't proud, not a mite. Besides, they've all seen Britishers afore.

MARY: I suppose you allude to my cousin, Edward Trenchard?

ASA: Well, he wan't the only one; there was the old Squire, Mark Trenchard.

MARY [*Starting aside*]: My grandfather!

ASA: Oh! He was a fine old hoss, as game as a bison bull, and as gray as a coon in the fall. You see he was kinder mad with his folks here; so he come over to America to look after the original branch of the family. That's our branch. We're older than the Trenchards on this side of the water. Yes, we've got the start of the heap.

MARY: Tell me, Mr. Trenchard, did he ever receive any letters from his daughter?

ASA: Oh, yes, lots of them; but the old cuss never read them, though. He chucked them in the fire as soon as he made out who they come from.

MARY [*Aside*]: My poor mother.

ASA: You see, as nigh as we could reckon it up, she had gone and got married agin his will, and that made him mad. And, well, he was a queer kind of a rusty fusty old coon, and it appeared that he got older, and rustier, and fustier, and coonier every fall. You see, it always took him in the fall; it was too much for him. He got took down with the ague, he was so bad the doctors gave him up, and mother she went for a minister. And while she was gone the old man called me in his room: 'Come in, Asa, boy', says he, and his voice rang loud and clear as a bell, 'come in', says he. I come in; 'Sit down', says he. Well, I sot down. You see, I was always a favorite with the old man. 'Asa, my boy', says he, takin' a great piece of paper, 'when I die, this sheet of paper makes you heir to all my property in England'. Well, you can calculate I pricked up my ears about that time. Bime-by the minister came, and I left the room, and I do believe he had a three day's fight with the devil, for that old man's soul, but he got the upper hand of Satan at last, and when the minister had gone the old man called me into his room again. The old Squire was sitting up in bed, his face as white as the sheet that covered him, his silken hair flowing in silvery locks from under his red cap, and the tears rolling from his large blue eyes down his furrowed cheek, like two mill streams. Will you excuse my lighting a cigar? For the story is long and awful moving, and I don't think I could get on without a smoke. *[Strikes match]* Wal, says he to me, and his voice was not as loud as it was afore—it was like the whisper of the wind in a pine forest, low and awful. 'Asa, boy', said he, 'I feel that I've been a wicked old sinner in hardening my heart against my own flesh and blood, but it is not too late to atone for the wrong I done; give me the light', says he. Wal I gave him the candle that stood by his bedside, and he took the sheet of paper I was telling you of, just as I might take this. *[Takes will from his pocket]* And he twisted it up as I might this, *[Lights will]* and he lit it just this way, and he watched it burn slowly and slowly away. Then, says he, 'Asa, boy, that act disinherits you, but it leaves all my property to one who has a better right to it. My own daughter's darling child, Mary Meredith', and then he smiled, sank back on his pillow, drew a long sigh as if he felt relieved, and that was the last of poor old Mark Trenchard.

MARY: Poor Grandfather! *[Buries her face and sobs]*

Asa *[After business]:*   Wal, I guess I'd better leave her alone. *[Sees half burned will]* There lies four hundred thousand dollars, if there's a cent. Asa, boy, you're a hoss. *[Starts off, right left center]*

MARY: To me, all to me. Oh, Mr. Trenchard, how we have all wronged poor Grandfather. What, gone? He felt after such tidings—he felt I should be left alone. Who would suspect there was such delicacy under that rough husk—but I can hardly believe the startling news—his heiress—I, the penniless orphan of an hour ago, no longer penniless, but, alas, an orphan still, *[Enter FLORENCE]* with none to share my wealth, none to love me.

FLORENCE *[Throwing arms around MARY's neck]:*   What treason is this, Mary? None to love you, eh? What's the matter? You've been weeping, and I met that American savage coming from here—he has not been rude to you?

MARY: Oh, no, he's the gentlest of human beings, but he has just told me news that has moved me strangely.

FLORENCE: What is it, love?

MARY: That all Grandfather's property is mine, mine—Florence, do you understand?

FLORENCE: What! He has proposed, has he? I thought he would.

MARY: What do you mean?

FLORENCE: Who? Asa Trenchard, to be sure.

MARY: Asa Trenchard? Why, what put that in your head?

FLORENCE: Why, how can Mark Trenchard's property be yours, unless you marry the legatee?

MARY: The legatee? Who?

FLORENCE: Why, you know Mark Trenchard left everything to Asa.

MARY: No, no, you have been misinformed.

FLORENCE: Nonsense; he showed it to me, not an hour ago on a half sheet of rough paper just like this. *[Sees will]* Like this. *[Picks it up]* Why, this is part of it, I believe.

MARY: That's the paper he lighted his cigar with.

FLORENCE: Then he lighted his cigar with 80,000 pounds. Here is old Mark Trenchard's signature.

MARY: Yes, I recognize the hand.

FLORENCE: And here are the words 'Asa Trenchard, in consideration of sole heir'—etc.—etc.—etc.

MARY: Oh, Florence, what does this mean?

FLORENCE: It means that he is a true hero, and he loves you, you little rogue. *[Embraces her]*

MARY: Generous man. *[Hides face in FLORENCE's bosom]*

FLORENCE: Oh, won't I tease him now! I'll find him at once. *[Runs off, right, MARY after her calling "Florence!! Florence!!' as scene closes. Curtain]*

Scene 2

Chamber in Trenchard Manor (same as in Act I, Scene 3).
Enter MRS. MOUNTCHESSINGTON and AUGUSTA, left.

MRS. MOUNT: Yes, my child, while Mr. de Boots and Mr. Trenchard are both here, you must ask yourself seriously, as to the state of your affections. Remember, your happiness for life will depend on the choice you make.

AUGUSTA: What would you advise, Mamma? You know I am always advised by you.

MRS. MOUNT: Dear, obedient child. de Boots has excellent expectations, but then they are only expectations after all. This American is rich, and on the whole I think a well regulated affection ought to incline to Asa Trenchard.

AUGUSTA: Very well, Mamma.

MRS. MOUNT: At the same time, you must be cautious, or in grasping at Asa Trenchard's solid good qualities, you may miss them—and de Boots's expectations into the bargain.

AUGUSTA: Oh, I will take care not to give up my hold on poor de Boots till I am quite sure of the American.

MRS. MOUNT: That's my own girl. *[Enter ASA, left]* Ah, Mr. Trenchard, we were just talking of your archery powers.

ASA: Wal, I guess shooting with bows and arrows is just like most things in life: all you've got to do is keep the sun out of your eyes, look straight, pull strong, calculate the distance, and let her rip.

AUGUSTA: But not in England, Mr. Trenchard. There are disinterested hearts that only ask an opportunity of showing how they despise that gold, which others set such store by.

ASA: Wal, I suppose there are, Miss Gusty.

AUGUSTA: All I crave is affection.

ASA *[Crosses to center]*:   Do you, now? I wish I could make sure of that, for I've been cruelly disappointed in that particular.

MRS. MOUNT: Yes, but we are old friends, Mr. Trenchard, and you needn't be afraid of us.

ASA: Oh, I ain't afraid of you—both on you together.

MRS. MOUNT: People sometimes look a great way off, for that which is near at hand. *[Glancing at AUGUSTA and ASA alternately]*

ASA: You don't mean Miss Gusta. *[AUGUSTA casts sheeps' eyes at him]* Now, don't look at me in that way. I can't stand it. If you do, I'll bust.

MRS. MOUNT: Oh, if you only knew how refreshing this ingenuousness of yours is to an old woman of the world like me.

ASA: Be you an old woman of the world?

MRS. MOUNT: Yes, sir.

AUGUSTA: Oh, yes.

ASA: Well, I don't doubt it in the least. *[Aside]* This gal and the old woman are trying to get me on a string. *[Aloud]* Wal, then if a rough spun fellow like me was to come forward as a suitor for your daughter's hand, you wouldn't treat me as some folks do, when they find out I wasn't heir to the fortune.

Mrs. Mount: Not heir to the fortune, Mr. Trenchard?

Asa: Oh, no.

Augusta: What, no fortune?

Asa: Nary red. It all comes to their barkin' up the wrong tree about the old man's property.

Mrs. Mount: Which he left to you.

Asa: Oh, no.

Augusta: Not to you?

Asa: No, which he meant to leave to me, but he thought better on it, and left it to his granddaughter, Miss Mary Meredith.

Mrs. Mount: Miss Mary Meredith! Oh, I'm delighted.

Augusta: Delighted?

Asa: Yes, you both look tickled to death. Now, some gals, and mothers, would go away from a fellow when they found that out, but you don't valley fortune, Miss Gusty?

Mrs. Mount *[Aside, crosses to Augusta]*:   My love, you had better go.

Asa: You crave affection, *you* do. Now I've no fortune, but I'm biling over with affections, which I'm ready to pour out to all of you, like apple sass over roast pork.

Mrs. Mount: Mr. Trenchard, you will please recollect you are addressing my daughter, and in my presence.

Asa: Yes, I'm offering her my heart and hand just as she wants them, with nothing in 'em.

Mrs. Mount: Augusta, dear, to your room.

Augusta: Yes, Ma, the nasty beast. *[Exit, right]*

Mrs. Mount: I am aware, Mr. Trenchard, you are not used to the manners of good society, and that, alone, will excuse the impertinence of which you have been guilty. *[Exit, left]*

Asa *[Calling after her]*:   Don't know the manners of good society, eh? Wal, I guess I know enough to turn you inside out, old gal—you sockdologizing old man-trap.[4] Wal, now, when I think

---

4. It was at this point, with Asa alone at stage left and the audience laughing, that Booth fired the fatal shot.

of what I've thrown away in hard cash today I'm apt to call my-self some awful hard names; 400,000 dollars is a big pile for a man to light his cigar with. If that gal had only given me herself in exchange, it wouldn't have been a bad bargain. But I dare no more ask that gal to be my wife, than I dare ask Queen Victoria to dance a Cape Cod reel.

Enter FLORENCE, *left.*

FLORENCE: What do you mean by doing all these dreadful things?

ASA: Which things?

FLORENCE: Come here, sir. *[He does so]*

ASA: What's the matter?

FLORENCE: Do you know this piece of paper? *[Showing burned paper]*

ASA: Well, I think I have seen it before. *[Aside]* It's old Mark Trenchard's will that I left half burned up, like a landhead that I am.

FLORENCE: And you're determined to give up this fortune to Mary Meredith.

ASA: Wal, I couldn't help it if I tried.

FLORENCE: Oh, don't say that.

ASA: I didn't mean to do it when I first come here—hadn't the least idea in the world of it. But when I saw that everlasting an-gel of a gal movin' around among them fixin's like a sunbeam in a shady place; and when I pictured her without a dollar in the world—I—well, my old Adam riz right up, and I said, 'Asa do it'—and I did it.

FLORENCE: Well, I don't know who your old Adam may be, but whoever it is, he's a very honest man to consult you to do so good an action. But how dare you do such an outrageous thing? You impudent—you unceremonious, oh! You unselfish man! You! You! You! *[Smothers him with kisses, and runs off, right]*

ASA: Wal, if that ain't worth four hundred thousand dollars, I don't know what is. It was sweeter than cider right out of the bung-hole. Let me see how things stand 'round here. Thanks to old whiskers I've got that ship for the sailor man, and that makes him and Miss Florence all hunk. Then there's that darned old Coyle. Wal, I guess me and old Murcott can fix his flint for him. Then there's—*[Looks off left]* Christopher Columbus, here comes Mary.

Enter Mary, left.

MARY: Mr. Trenchard, what can I say to you but offer you my life-long gratitude?

ASA: Don't now, Miss, don't—*[Turns away, twice]*

MARY: If I knew what else to offer, Heaven knows there is nothing that is mine to give that I would keep back.

ASA: Give me yourself. *[Business]* I know what a rude, ill-mannered block I am; but there's a heart inside of me worth something, if it's only for the sake of your dear little image, that's planted right plumb in the middle of it.

MARY: Asa Trenchard, there is my hand, and my heart is in it.

ASA *[Seizes her hand, then drops it suddenly]*: Miss Mary, I made what folks call a big sacrifice for you this morning. Oh! I know it; I ain't so modest but that I know it. Now, what's this you're doing? Is this sacrifice you're making out of gratitude for me? 'Cause if it is, I wouldn't have it, though not to have it would nigh break my heart, tough as it is.

MARY: No, no, I give myself freely to you—as freely as you, this morning, gave my grandfather's property to me.

ASA: God bless you, Mary! *[Clasps her in his arms]* There's something tells me that you'll not repent it. I may be a rough specimen of a man, Miss Mary, but you needn't fear that I'll ever be rough to you. I've camped out in the woods, Mary, and seen the wild bear who in her savage fury would tear the bold hunter piecemeal, as gentle and loving to her young as a mother to her child. I've seen that claw that would peel a man's head, as a knife would open a pumpkin, as gentle to them as if it was made of velvet. Which I'll be with you, Mary. And if ever harm should reach you, it must come over the dead body of Asa Trenchard.

MARY: I know it, Asa. And if I do not prove a true and loving wife to you, may my mother's bright spirit never look down to bless her child.

ASA: Wal, if I don't get out in the air, I'll bust. *[Exit hastily, right, pulling Mary after him]*

Enter Binny, left, drunk.

BINNY *[Calling]*: Mr. H'Asa, Mr. H'Asa! Oh, he's gone; well, I suppose he'll come back to keep his happointment. Mr. Coyle's quite impatient. It isn't hoften that han hamerican has the run of the wine cellars of Trenchard Manor, and in such company, too. There's me and Mr. Coyle, which is a good judge of old port wine, and he knows it when he drinks. And his clerk, Mr. Murcott, which I don't hexactly like sitting down with clerks. But Mr. H'Asa wished it and Mr. Coyle hadn't any objections; so in course I put my feelings in my pocket. Besides, Murcott is a man of hedication, though unfortunately taken to drink. Well, what of that? It's been many a man's misfortune, though I say it, what shouldn't say it, being a butler. But now to join my distinguished party. *[Exit, right. Curtain]*

Scene 3

Wine cellar in Trenchard Manor.
COYLE, MURCOTT, and BINNY discovered. Table, left, with two cups and bottles. COYLE left of table, seated. BINNY back of table. MURCOTT sitting on barrel, right. Door in flat with staircase discovered, dark. Stage half dark. Candles on table, lighted.

COYLE: A capital glass of wine, Mr. Binny, and a capital place to drink it.

ASA *[Without]*: Bring a light here, can't you? I've broken my natural allowance of shins already. *[Enters down in front, down stairs. To MURCOTT]*: Is he tight yet?

MURCOTT: No, but I think another glass or two will settle him.

ASA: That's all right, but mind you don't touch a drop yourself.

COYLE: Oh, Mr. Trenchard, glad to see you—to welcome you to the vaults of our ancestors.

ASA: Oh! These are the vaults of my ancestors, are they? Wal, you seem to be punishing their spirits pretty well.

BINNY: Wines, Mr. H'Asa. The spirits are in the houter cellar.

COYLE: Oh, Mr. Asa, there is no place like a wine cellar for a hearty bout. Here you might bawl yourself hoarse beneath these ribs of stone, and nobody hear you. *[He shouts and sings very loud]*

ASA: Oh, wouldn't they hear you? *[Aside]* That's worth knowing.

BINNY *[Very drunk, rising]*: That's right, Mr. Coyle, make as much noise as you like, you are in the cellars of Trenchard Manor, Mr. Coyle. Mr. Coyle, bless you, Mr. Coyle. Mr. Coyle, why his hit, Mr. Coyle, I am sitting at the present time, in this present distinguished company? I will tell you, Mr. Coyle, hit his because Hi always hacts and conducts myself has becomes a gentleman, hand Hi knows what's due to manners. *[Falls on chair]*

Asa: Steady, old hoss, steady.

Binny: Hi'm steady. Hi always was steady. *[Staggers across to left]* Hi'm going to fetch clean glasses. *[Exit, left]*

Asa: Now, Mr. Coyle, suppose you give us a song.

Coyle *[Very drunk]*: I can't sing, Mr. Trenchard, but I sometimes join in the chorus.

Asa: Wal, give us a chorus.

Coyle: Will you assist in the vocalization thereof?

Asa *[Mimicking]*: Will do the best of my endeavors thereunto.

Coyle *[Sings]*: 'We won't go home till morning'. *[Repeats] [Repeats again. Falls off chair, senseless]*

Asa *[Finishing the strain]*: 'I don't think you'll go home at all'. Now, then, quick, Murcott, before the butler comes back, get his keys. *[Murcott gets keys from Coyle's pocket and throws them to Asa]* Is this all?

Murcott: No, the key to his private bureau is on his watch chain, and I can't get it off.

Asa: Take the watch and all.

Murcott: No, he will accuse me of robbing him.

Asa: Never mind; I'll take the responsibility. *[Coyle moves]*

Murcott: He is getting up.

Asa: Wal, darn me. Knock him down again.

Murcott: I can't.

Asa: Can't you? Wal, I can.

Pulls Murcott away. knocks Coyle down; is passing down front as he meets Binny with tray and glasses; collides with it, knocking Binny down; exits up staircase, followed by Murcott, carrying candle. Dark stage. Binny rises; Coyle ditto. Blindly encounter each other and pummel soundly till curtain.

Scene 4

Library in Trenchard Manor.
Enter Dundreary and Vernon, left. Dundreary stops, center, and is seized with an inclination to sneeze. Motions with his hand to Vernon.

VERNON: My lord! *[Business of DUNDREARY sneezing]* Your lordship! *[Same DUNDREARY business again, only louder]* My lord!

DUNDREARY: There you go; now you've spoiled it.

VERNON: Spoiled what, my lord?

DUNDREARY: Spoiled what? Why, a most magnificent sneeze.

VERNON: I'm very sorry to interrupt your lordship's sneeze, but I merely wanted to express my gratitude to you for getting me a ship.

DUNDREARY: Sir, I don't want your gratitude; I only want to sneeze.

VERNON: Very well, my lord, then I will leave you, and thus give you an opportunity for sneezing. *[Crosses to right]* But in return for what you have done for me, should you ever want a service a sailor can offer you, just hail Harry Vernon, and you'll find he'll weigh anchor and be alongside. *[Hitches up breeches and exits, right]*

DUNDREARY: Find him alongside? What does he mean by a long side? And he always wants to weigh anchor. What funny fellows the sailors are. Why the devil don't they keep a memorandum of the weight of their anchor? What's the matter with the sailor's side? *[Imitates VERNON]* Oh, I see. He's got a stomach ache. *[Exit, right]*

Enter BUDDICOMBE, right.

BUDDICOMBE: A Letter, my lord.

DUNDREARY *[Takes letter]:* You may go. *[Exit BUDDICOMBE, right]* What a small letter to come over in such a big steamer. Who is it from?

VERNON: The best plan I can suggest of arriving at that information, my lord, is to open it and see. *[Exit, right]*

DUNDREARY: As if any fool didn't know that. *[Reads back of envelope]* 'If you don't get this letter, write and let me know'. *[Laughs]* Well, that fellow's an ass, whoever he is. I don't know anybody in America except Sam. Of course I know Sam because he's my brother. Every fellow knows his brother. *[Laughs]* Sam and I used to be boys when we were lads, both of us—we were always together. *[Laughs]* People used to say 'Birds of a feather'—what is it birds of a feather do?—Oh, 'Birds of a feather gather no moss'. That's ridiculous—fancy a lot of birds going about picking up moss. Oh, no—it's the 'early bird', that's what it is, 'that knows its own father'. That's worse than the other. Oh, no—'It's the wise child', that's what it is—'the wise child that gets the worms— *[Laughs]* Oh, that's worse than any of them. I don't believe that any parent would allow its child to go about picking up a lot of worms . . . besides, the whole proverb's nonsense from beginning to end. 'Birds of a feather'—as if the whole flock of birds had only one feather. Why, they'd catch cold—every one of them. Besides, there's only one of these birds could have that feather, and he'd fly all on one side. Oh, no, it's rhyme. That's what it is. 'Birds of a feather flock together'. No bird would be such a damned fool as to go into a corner and flock all by himself—Oh, that's one of those things no fellow can find out. *[Looks at letter]* Whoever it's from, he's written it upside down—*[Laughs]* Oh, no, I've got it upside down. I knew some fellow was upside down. *[Laughs. Opens letter]* Yes, this is from Sam. I always know Sam's handwriting—when I see his name on the other side—'America'. Well, I'm glad he sent me the address. 'My dear Brother—' *[Laughs]* Sam always calls me brother, because neither of us have got any sister. 'My dear brother: I fear my last letter miscarried—as I was in such a hurry for the post I forgot to put my address on the envelope'. Well, I suppose that's the reason I never got it, then. Who could have got it? The postman couldn't go about asking every fellow he met if he'd got no name. Sam's an ass, Sam is. 'I find out now'—*[Laughs]* What's he found out now? 'I find out now that I was changed at my birth'. Now, what damned nonsense that is—why didn't he find out before? 'My old nurse turns out to be my mother'. Now, what rubbish that is! Well, if that's true all I can say is—Sam isn't my brother, and if Sam isn't my brother, then who the devil am I—Stop a moment. *[Rises]* If Sam's old nurse turns out to be his mother, *my* mother—my mother will turn out to be some other fellow's old nurse! Stop a moment! Let's see . . . how is that? *[With right hand pushes up index finger of left]* That's Sam's mother. *[With right hand pushes up thumb of left]* That's Sam's nurse. Sam's nurse is only half the size of his mother. Well, that's *my* mother!—That's my mother . . . Hang it! *[With right hand tries to make third finger of left hand stand up]* I can't get my mother to stand up. I never had such a stupid mother as that. *[Holds up middle finger of right hand and opens up left hand]* Well, that's my mother. *[Looking at opened left hand]*

Hello, there's a whole lot of other fellows' mothers. As far as I can make it out Sam's got five or six mothers, confound him. He hasn't left me any mother at all... Then the point is, who's my father? Oh, that's one of those thing no fellow can find out. *[Exits, left. Re-enters after applause]*[5]

DUNDREARY returns, in response to applause.

DUNDREARY *[Reads]:* 'P.S. By the bye what do you think of the following riddle'? Sam's always asking riddles, and I hate riddles. 'If 14 dogs with 3 legs each catch 48 rabbits with 76 legs in 25 minutes'—I shall have a fit in a moment. '... How many legs must 24 rabbits have to get away from 3,000 dogs with no legs at all?' *[Exits, left]*

Re-enters after more applause.

DUNDREARY: 'P.S.'—Sam's a devil of a fellow for his P.Ss—'You will be glad to hear I've purchased a large estate'. I'm glad to hear that. '... Somewhere or other'—Sam evidently knows where it is... Oh, yes! '... Somewhere or another on the banks of the Missi-ssippi'. *[Laughs]* Sam's getting on well in America! '... Send me the purchase money'—*[Business]* 'The enclosed pill box'—*[Shakes letter and looks about for pill box]* Where the devil's the pill box? '... The enclosed pill box contains a sample of the soil'. *[Business and exit, left. Curtain]*

Scene 5

COYLE'S Office. High desk and stool, right. Modern box center rear; cabinet, left.
ASA discovered looking over papers on box; MURCOTT looking in desk.

ASA: Have you found it?

MURCOTT: No, Mr. Trenchard. I've searched all the drawers but can find no trace of it.

ASA: What's this?

---

5. E. A. SOTHERN'S NOTE: Asa and Murcott are ready to come on in case Dundreary does not read P.Ss (ad-lib postscripts to Sam's letter)

MURCOTT: That's a cabinet where his father kept old deeds; the key he always carries about with him.

ASA: Oh, he does, does he? Wal, I reckon I saw a key as I came in that will open it. *[Exit, right]*

MURCOTT: Key! Oh, my poor muddled brain, what can he mean!

ASA *[Re-enters with axe]*:   Here's a key that will open any lock that Hobb ever invented.

MURCOTT: Key? What key?

ASA: What key? Why, Yankee. *[Shows axe. Begins to break open cabinet]*

Enter COYLE, *right.*

COYLE: Villains! Would you rob me?

MURCOTT: Stand off, Mr. Coyle, we are desperate. *[Seizes him]*

ASA: Here it is as sure as there are snakes in Virginia. Let the old cuss go, Murcott.

COYLE: Burglars! Oh, you shall pay dearly for this.

ASA: Yes, I'll pay—but I guess you'll find the change.

COYLE: The law—the law shall aid me.

ASA: Wal, perhaps it would be as well not to call in the law just yet. It might look a little further than might be convenient.

MURCOTT: It's no use to blunder, Mr. Coyle; you are harmless to me now, for we have that will crush you.

COYLE: Well, what are your conditions? Money? How much?

ASA: Wal, we weren't thinking of coming down on your dollars. But you have an appointment with Sir Edward at two, haven't you?

COYLE: Well?

ASA: Wal, I want you to keep that appointment.

COYLE: Keep it?

ASA: Yes, and that's all I do want you to keep of his, and instead of saying you have come to foreclose on the mortgage, I want you to say you have found the release which proves the mortgage to have been paid off.

COYLE: I accept. Is that all?

ASA: Not quite. Then I want you to pay off the execution debts.

COYLE: What, I pay Sir Edward's debts?

ASA: Yes, with Sir Edward's money that stuck to your fingers naturally while passing through your hands.

COYLE *[To MURCOTT]:* Traitor!

MURCOTT: He knows all, Mr. Coyle.

COYLE: Is there anything more?

ASA: Yes, I want you to apologize to Miss Florence Trenchard, for having the darned impudence to propose for her hand.

COYLE: I consent.

ASA: Then resign your stewardship in favor of your clerk, Abel Murcott.

COYLE: What, that drunkard vagabond?

ASA: Wal, he was, but he's going to take the pledge at the first pump he comes to.

MURCOTT: Yes, I *will* conquer the demon drink, or die in the struggle with him.

COYLE: Well, anything more?

ASA: Yes, I think the next thing will be to get washed. You're not a handsome man at the best, and now you're awful. *[COYLE makes a dash at MURCOTT. ASA catches him and turns him around to right]* Mr. Coyle, in your present state of mind, you had better go first.

COYLE *[Bitterly]:* Oh, sir, it is your turn now.

ASA: Yes, it is my turn, but you can have the first wash. Come along, Murcott. *[Exeunt]*

Scene 6

Library in Trenchard Manor.
SIR EDWARD discovered seated right of table.

SIR EDWARD: The clock is on the stroke of two, and Coyle is waiting my decision. In giving her to him, I know I shall be embittering her life to save my fortune, but appearances—no, no, I will not sacrifice her young life so full of promise for a few short years of questionable state for myself. Better leave her to the mercy of chance *[Enter FLORENCE, right]* than sell her to this scoundrel. And to myself, I will not survive the downfall of my house, but end it thus. *[Raises pistol to his head. FLORENCE seizes his arms and screams]*

FLORENCE: Father, dear Father, what despair is this? *[SIR EDWARD buries his head in his hands]* If it is fear of poverty, do not think of me. I will marry this man if I drop dead in my bridal robes.

Enter BINNY, right.

BINNY: Mr. Coyle, sir, who has come by happointment.

SIR EDWARD: I will not see him.

FLORENCE: Yes, yes, show him up, Mr. Binny. *[Exit BINNY, right]*

SIR EDWARD: Florence, I will not consent to this sacrifice.

Enter ASA, COYLE, and MURCOTT, right.

SIR EDWARD: How is this, Mr. Coyle? You are not alone?

ASA: No, you see, Squire, Mr. Coyle wishes me and his clerk to witness the cutting off the seals from the mortgage, which he has been lucky enough to find the release of.

SIR EDWARD: Heavens, is it so?

COYLE: Yes, Sir Edward, there is the release executed by my father, which had become detached.

ASA *[To him]*: Accidentally.

SIR EDWARD: Saved, saved at last from want!

COYLE: Meanwhile I have paid the execution debts out of a fine which has just fallen in.

ASA: Accidentally. It's astonishing how things have fallen in and out today.

SIR EDWARD: But your demand here? *[Points to FLORENCE]*

COYLE: I make none, Sir Edward. I regret that I should have conceived so mad a thought; it is enough to unfit me for longer holding position as your agent, which I beg humbly to resign.

ASA *[Aside to him]*: Recommending as your successor . . .

COYLE: . . . Recommending as my successor Abel Murcott, whose knowledge of your affairs, gained in my office, will render him as useful as I have been.

ASA: Yes, just about.

SIR EDWARD: Your request is granted, Mr. Coyle.

ASA: And now, my dear Mr. Coyle, you may ab-squa-tu-late.

COYLE: I go, Sir Edward, with equal good wishes for all assembled here. *[Darts a look at MURCOTT and exits, right]*

ASA: That's a good man, Sir Edward.

SIR EDWARD: Yes.

ASA: Oh, he's a very good man.

SIR EDWARD: Yes, he's a good man.

ASA: But he can't keep a hotel.

SIR EDWARD: Mr. Murcott, your offense was heavy.

FLORENCE: And so has been his reparation. Forgive him, Papa. Mr. Murcott, you saved me. May heaven bless you.

MURCOTT: Yes, I saved her, thank heaven. I had strength enough for that. *[Exit, left]*

FLORENCE: You'll keep your promise, and make Mr. Murcott your clerk, Papa?

SIR EDWARD: Yes, I can refuse nothing; I am so happy; I am so happy I can refuse none anything today.

ASA: Can't you, Sir Edward? Now, that's awful lucky, for there's two gals want your consent mighty bad.

SIR EDWARD: Indeed. For what?

ASA: To get hitched.

SIR EDWARD: Hitched?

ASA: Yes, to get spliced.

SIR EDWARD: Spliced?

ASA: Yes, to get married.

SIR EDWARD: They have it by anticipation. Who are they?

ASA: There's one on 'em. *[Points to* FLORENCE*]*

SIR EDWARD: Florence! And the other?

ASA: She's right outside. *[Exits, hastily, right]*

SIR EDWARD: Well, and who is the happy man, Lord Dun—

FLORENCE: Lord Dundreary! No, Papa—but Harry Vernon. He's not poor now, though. He's got a ship.

Re-enter ASA, *with* MARY.

ASA: Here's the other one, Sir Edward.

SIR EDWARD: Mary? Who is the object of your choice?

MARY: Rough-spun, honest-hearted Asa Trenchard.

SIR EDWARD: Ah! Mr. Trenchard, you win a heart of gold.

FLORENCE: And so does Mary, Papa. Believe me. *[Crosses to* ASA. MARY *and* SIR EDWARD *go up]*

FLORENCE: What's the matter?

ASA: You make me blush.

FLORENCE: I don't see you blushing.

ASA: I'm blushing all the way down my back.

FLORENCE: Oh, you go 'long. *[Goes up stage]*

ASA: Hello! Here's all the folks coming two by two, as if they were pairing for Noah's ark. Here's Mrs. Mountchestnut and the sailor man. *[Enter as ASA calls them off]* Here's de Boots and his gal, and darn me if here ain't old setidy fetch it, and the sick gal. How are you, Buttons? *[DUNDREARY knocks against ASA at stage center]*

DUNDREARY: There's that darned rhinocerous again. *[Crosses to left with GEORGINA; seats her]*

ASA: Here comes Turkey Cock number two and his gal and, darn me, if here ain't Puffy and his gal.

SIR EDWARD: Vernon, take her. She's yours, though heaven knows what I shall do without her.

MRS. MOUNT *[Rising]*:   Ah, Sir Edward, that is just my case; but you'll never know what it is to be a mother. *[Comes down, left center]* Georgina, Augusta, my dears, come here. *[They come down each side of her]* You'll sometimes think of dear Mamma, bless you. *[Aside to them]* Oh, you couple of fools. *[Bumps their foreheads together]*

DUNDREARY *has business with* GEORGINA, *then leads her to a seat, left.*

DE BOOTS *[To DUNDREARY]*:   Why, Fred, we're all getting married!

DUNDREARY: Yes, it's catching, like the cholera.

BINNY: I 'ope, Sir Edward, there's no objections to my leading Miss Sharpe to the hymeneal halter.

SIR EDWARD: Certainly not, Mr. Binny.

BUDDICOMBE *[To DUNDREARY]*:   And Skillet and I have made so bold, My lord—

SIR EDWARD: Yes, you generally do make bold—but bless you, my children—bless you.

ASA: Say, you, Lord Buttons . . . I say, Whiskers.

DUNDREARY: Illustrious exile? *[Comes down]*

ASA: They're a nice color now. *[Touches his whiskers]*

DUNDREARY: Yes. They're all wight now.

ASA: All *wight?* No, they're all black.

DUNDREARY: When I say wight I mean black.

ASA: Say, shall I tell that sick gal about that hair dye?

DUNDREARY: No, *[Mimicking him]* you needn't tell that sick gal about that hair dye!

ASA: Wal, I won't, if you don't want me to.

DUNDREARY *[Aside]*: That man is a damned rattlesnake. *[Goes up, sits in GEORGINA'S lap. Same business with MRS. MOUNTCHESSINGTON. Then goes back to GEORGINA]*

ASA: Miss Georgina. *[She comes down]* How's your appetite? Shall I tell the lord about the beefsteak and onions I saw you pitching into?

GEORGINA: Please don't, Mr. Trenchard. I'm *so* delicate.

ASA: Wal, I won't, if you don't want me to.

GEORGINA: Oh, thank you. *[Backs up stage and sits in lap of Dundreary, who has taken her seat]*

ASA: Miss Gusty. *[AUGUSTA comes down]* Got your boots, hain't you?

AUGUSTA: Yes, Mr. Trenchard.

ASA: How do they fit you? Say, shall I tell that fellow you were after me first?

AUGUSTA: *[Extravagantly]*: Not for the world, Mr. Trenchard.

ASA *[Mimicking her]*: Wal, I won't, if you don't want me to.

ASA *[To MRS. MOUNTCHESSINGTON]*: Mrs. Mountchestnut.

DUNDREARY *[Coming down]*: Sir, I haven't a chestnut to offer you, but if you'd like some of your native food, I'll order you a doughnut.

ASA: I dough not see it.

DUNDREARY *[Laughs]*: That's good.

ASA: Yes, very good.

DUNDREARY: For you.

ASA: Oh, you get out—I mean the old lady.

DUNDREARY: Mrs. Mountchessington, this illustrious exile wishes to see you. *[MRS. MOUNTCHESSINGTON comes down]*

ASA: Wal, old woman.

MRS. MOUNT: Old woman, sir?

ASA: Got them two gals off your hands, haven't you?

MRS. MOUNT: I'm proud to say I have.

ASA: Shall I tell them fellows you tried to stick them on me first?

MRS. MOUNT: You'll please not mention the subject.

ASA: Wal, I won't, if you don't want me to. *[She backs up, curtseying; knocks against DUNDREARY, who is stooping to pick up a handkerchief. They turn and bump foreheads]* Say, Mr. Puffy *[BINNY comes down]* Shall I tell Sir Edward about your getting drunk in the wine cellar?

BINNY: You need not—not if you don't like unto.

ASA: Wal, I won't, if you don't want me to.

BINNY: Remember the old hadage: 'A still tongue is a wise 'ead'.

ASA: X. Q's me.

BINNY: O.I.C.

FLORENCE *[Comes down]:*   Well, cousin, what have you to say to us? *[MARY comes down right of ASA]*

ASA: Wal, I ain't got no ring to put in our noses, but I've got one to put on your finger. *[To MARY]* And I guess the sailor man has got one to put on yours, and I guess you two are happy as clams at high water.

FLORENCE: I am sure you must be very happy.

ASA: Wal, I am not so sure about my happiness.

FLORENCE: Why, you ungrateful fellow. What do you want to complete it?

ASA *[To audience]:*   My happiness depends on you.

FLORENCE: And I am sure you will not regret the kindness you have shown to Our American Cousin. But don't go yet, pray—for Lord Dundreary has a word to say. Dundreary! Dundreary!

DUNDREARY *[Sneezes]:*   That's the idea!

Curtain.

Appendix A

CAST OF CHARACTERS
Laura Keene's Theatre, New York, October 15, 1858

Lord Dundreary	Mr. E. A. Sothern
Asa Trenchard.......................	'' Jos. Jefferson
Sir Edward Trenchard.............	'' E[dwin] Varrey
Captain de Boots...................	'' Clinton
Harry Vernon	'' [Milnes] Levick
Abel Murcott........................	'' C. W. Couldock
Mr. Coyle............................	'' J. G. Burnett
Mr. Buddicombe....................	'' McDonall
Mr. Binny............................	'' [Charles] Peters
John Wickens	'' [B.] Brown
Mrs. Mountchessington...........	Miss Mary Wells
Florence Trenchard................	'' Laura Keene
Mary.................................	'' Sara Stevens
Augusta	'' E[ffie] Germon
Georgina.............................	Mrs. [E. A.] Sothern
Sharpe................................	Miss Flynn
Skillet................................	Mrs. M. Levick

Appendix B

CAST OF CHARACTERS
Ford's Theatre, Washington, D.C., April 14, 1865

Abel Murcott......................John Dyott

Asa Trenchard.....................Harry Hawk

Sir Edward Trenchard...........T[homas] C. Gourley[1]

Lord Dundreary ....E. A. Emerson

Mr. Coyle...........................J. Matthews

Lieutenant Vernon, R.N..........W[illiam] J. Ferguson

Captain de Boots..................C. Byrnes

Binny................................G. G. Spear

Buddicomb ....J. H. Evans

John Wickens[2] ....J. L. De Bonay

Bailiffs..............................G. A. Parkhurst and L. Johnson

Mary Meredith[3] ....Miss J[eannie] Gourley

Mrs. Mountchessington...........Mrs. H. Muzzy

Augusta ....Miss H[elen] Trueman

Georgina[4] ....Miss M. Hart

Sharpe.............................Mrs. J. H. Evans

Skillet..............................Miss Margaret
                                              Gourley

---

1. "Gourlay" on Ford's playbill
2. "Whicker" on Ford's playbill
3. "Mary Trenchard" on Ford's playbill
4. "Georgiana" on Ford's playbill

Appendix C

Because of the North's anti-British stance during the Civil War *Punch,* the satirical English weekly with which Tom Taylor was associated, satirized Lincoln frequently and at times mercilessly. Three weeks after his death the magazine attempted to atone for the liberties it had taken by means of an *amende honorable.* It consisted of a sketch, "Britannia Sympathizes with Columbia," by staff artist John Tenniel (see illustrations), who had often drawn outlandish cartoons of Lincoln, and a poem, "Abraham Lincoln," one of the most fervent poetic tributes to the slain President.

Some sources (e.g. Carl Sandburg) give Tom Taylor as the author of these lines, and some title them "Retraction." However, Marion H. Spielmann in his *History of Punch* identifies the author as Shirley Brooks, a long-time member of the editorial staff and subsequently head editor from 1870 until his death in 1874, when Tom Taylor succeeded to the post. The following is the original *Punch* text of May 6, 1865.

Abraham Lincoln
Foully Assassinated, April 14, 1865

You lay a wreath on murdered Lincoln's bier
   You, who with mocking pencil wont to trace,
Broad for the self-complacent British sneer,
   His length of shambling limb, his furrowed face,

His gaunt, gnarled hands, his unkempt, bristling hair,
   His garb uncouth, his bearing ill at ease,
His lack of all we prize as debonair,
   Of power or will to shine, of art to please.

You, whose smart pen backed up the pencil's laugh,
   Judging each step, as though the way were plain:
Reckless, so it could point its paragraph,
   Of chief's perplexity, or people's pain.

Beside this corpse, that bears for winding sheet
   The stars and stripes he lived to rear anew,
Between the mourners at his head and feet,
   Say, scurril-jester, is there room for you?

Yes, he had lived to shame me from my sneer,
   To lame my pencil, and confute my pen—
To make me own this hind of princes peer,
   This rail-splitter a true-born king of men.

My shallow judgment I had learned to rue,
   Noting how to occasions's height he rose,
How his quaint wit made home-truth seem more true,
   How, iron-like, his temper grew by blows.

How humble yet how hopeful he could be:
   How in good fortune and in ill the same:
Nor bitter in success, nor boastful he,
   Thirsty for gold, nor feverish for fame.

He went about his work—such work as few
   Ever had laid on head and heart and hand—
As one who knows, when there's a task to do,
   Man's honest will must Heaven's good grace command;

Who trusts the strength will with the burden grow
   That God makes instruments to work His will,
If but that will he can arrive to know,
   Nor tamper with the weights of good and ill.

So he went forth to battle, on the side
   That he felt clear was Liberty's and Right's,
As in his peasant boyhood he had plied
   His warfare with rude Nature's thwarting mights—

The uncleared forest, the unbroken soil,
   The iron-bark, that turns the lumberer's axe,
The rapid, that o'erbears the boatman's toil,
   The prairie, hiding the maz'd wanderer's tracks,

The ambushed Indians, and the prowling bear—
  Such were the needs that helped his youth to train:
Rough culture—but such trees large fruit may bear,
  If but their stocks be of right girth and grain.

So he grew up, a destined work to do,
  And lived to do it: four long suffering years'
Ill-fate, ill-feeling, ill-report, lived through,
  And then he heard the hisses change to cheers,

The taunts to tribute, the abuse to praise,
  And took both with the same unwavering mood:
Till, as he came on light, from darkling days,
  And seemed to touch the goal from where he stood,

A felon hand, between the goal and him,
  Reached from behind his back, a trigger prest,—
And those perplext and patient eyes were dim,
  Those gaunt, long-labouring limbs were laid to rest!

The words of mercy were upon his lips,
  Forgiveness in his heart and on his pen,
When this vile murderer brought swift eclipse
  To thoughts of peace on earth, good-will to men.

The Old World and the New, from sea to sea,
  Utter one voice of sympathy and shame!
Sore heart, so stopped when it at last beat high,
  Sad life, cut short just as its triumph came.

A Deed accurst! Strokes have been struck before
  By the assassin's hand, whereof men doubt
If more of horror or disgrace they bore;
  But thy foul crime, like CAIN's, stands darkly out,

Vile hand, that brandest murder on a strife,
  Whate'er its grounds, stoutly and nobly striven;
And with the martyr's crown crownest a life
  With much to praise, little to be forgiven!

SELECTED BIBLIOGRAPHY

Bishop, Jim. *The Day Lincoln Was Shot.* New York: Harper and Brothers, 1955.

Bryan, George S. *The Great American Myth.* New York: Harper and Brothers, 1940.

Buckingham, J. E. *Reminiscences and Souvenirs of the Assassination of Abraham Lincoln.* Washington, D.C.: Press of Rufus H. Darby, 1894.

Clark, Allen C. *Abraham Lincoln in the National Capital.* Washington: D.C.: Press of J. H. Roberts, 1925.

Creehan, John. *The Life of Laura Keene.* Philadelphia: The Rodgers Publishing Company, 1897.

Ferguson, W. J. *I Saw Booth Shoot Lincoln.* Boston: Houghton Mifflin Company, 1930.

Ford, George D. *These Were Actors.* New York: Library Publishers, 1955.

Grover, Leonard. "Lincoln's Interest in the Theatre." *Century Magazine* 73 (April 1909): 943–50.

Harbin, Billy J. "Laura Keene at the Lincoln Assassination." *Educational Theatre Journal* 18(March 1966): 47–54.

Hornblow, Arthur. *A History of the Theatre in America from Its Beginnings to the Present Time.* 2 vols. Philadelphia: J. B. Lippincott and Co., 1919.

Hughes, Glenn. *A History of the American Theatre.* New York: Samuel French, 1951.

Jefferson, Joseph. *Autobiography.* Edited by Alan Downer. Cambridge, Mass.: Harvard Univ. Press, 1964.

Laughlin, Clara E. *The Death of Lincoln.* New York: Doubleday, Page, 1909.

Olszewski, George J. *Restoration of Ford's Theatre.* Washington, D.C.: U.S. Government Printing Office, 1963.

Pemberton, T[homas] Edgar. *A Memoir of Edward Askew Sothern.* London: Richard Bentley and Son, 1889.

Quinn, Arthur Hobson. *A History of American Drama from the Beginning to the Civil War.* New York: Harper and Brothers, 1923.

Rose, Sidney. "Our American Cousin." *Variety* 206 (January 5, 1966): 10, 40.

Sandburg, Carl. *Abraham Lincoln: The War Years,* Vol IV. New York: Harcourt, Brace & Co., 1939.

Seaton, Munroe. "Recollections of Lincoln's Assassination. *North American Review* 163(April 1896): 424–34.

Shepard, Julia Adelaide. "Lincoln's Assassination Told by an Eye-Witness." *Century Magazine* 73 (April, 1909): 917–18.

Spielmann, M[arion] H[arry]. *The History of 'Punch'.* London: Cassell and Company, Ltd., 1895. Reprint, New York: Greenwood Press, 1969.

Tidwell, William A., et als. *Come Retribution: The Confederate Secret Service and the Assassination of Lincoln.* Jackson [Miss.] and London: University Press of Mississippi, 1988.

Tolles, Winton. *Tom Taylor and the Victorian Drama.* New York: Columbia Univ. Press, 1940.

Wilson, Francis. *John Wilkes Booth—Fact and Fiction of Lincoln's Assassination.* New York: Houghton Mifflin, 1929.

Winter, William. *Other Days: Being Chronicles and Memories of the Stage.* New York: Moffot, Yard, and Co., 1908.